Over 40 Survival Dating Guide

As if dating wasn't hard enough, let's add a pandemic!

Copyright © 2021 by RTG Books LLC

All rights reserved. No part of this publication may be reproduced, distributed, or transmitted in any form or by any means, including photocopying, recording, or other electronic or mechanical methods, without the prior written permission of the publisher, except in the case of brief quotations embodied in critical reviews and certain other noncommercial uses permitted by copyright law.

For permission requests, write to the author, addressed "Attention: Permissions Coordinator," at the Internet address - RTG.Books@gmail.com

About this guide

Greetings Sly Fox. This guide is meant to provide some humor while navigating the dating scene during this lovely pandemic. It contains useful information conveyed in a thought-provoking way while trying to cover the outlandish multitude of dating definitions of today. In addition to all of that, a straightforward, pseudo formula-based system on how to select a potential partner has been included. All of this awesomeness combines for a fun review of some dating stories. Of course, the stories and opinions expressed here are based solely on my experiences, and may or may not apply to everyone. Have fun, good luck, and be safe out there.

Contents

Hello Pandemic 4

Modus operandi 10

Transparency types..11

Drama factor 17

Grey area of Liars and Ass Fuckery 21

Lost Art of Manners and the Wandering Eye of Shithead 25

Health..29

Vegas Baby 37

Hot Mess Factor..40

Hygiene Anyone..44

Financial Savvy...48

Personality test / S.T.A.R...56

PADTFM, Oh My 59

STI -STD – WTF 63

The X 67

Social Media..70

Bi-Nuclear or Blended 73

Sly Fox, Get the Data...76

Background Checkup 78

Red Flags 81

We Actually Do Shit 83

Work the Formula 99

Wrap Up 113

Hello Pandemic

Congratulations, you have made it into your 40's. Life has surely given you a taste of what you like and unfortunately some things you didn't. After having ultimate fun dating in your 40's, lets add a pandemic to really make it challenging. But hey, stay positive, you got this. This dating survival guide is meant to help maximize your valuable time and hopefully provide a few techniques on identifying red flags while pseudo-dating (during and post) this pandemic, before you are forced to experience them firsthand. I have filled the guide with informative sections that we will step through together. It also includes tips on how to get the data needed to make the decision to "*move on*" or "*jump on*".

Oh, how I miss the shitty times

Back in the day, one could simply hit the club or the bar with friends, and bingo, target rich environment. No problem. Or remember the times when you could use the safety of a group hangout to pick up someone new and if it didn't provide results it was still okay because you were already having a blast with your friends anyway? Well, those days seem to have vanished and have been replaced with limited lockdown work-related functions and/or family events. And if you have children, it's even worse. Time is a precious thing now and wasting it on a jerk was so "Pre-COVID". Not much has changed on that front. COVID-19 still offers the same jerk interfacing. The difference is that it now comes with face masks, lonely social-killjoy lockdowns, and a doomsday news cycle of insanity. I've already watched all my favorite shows and now I'm re-watching them during the on again, off again '*stay at home*' orders. With this lonesome cycle, I had to rethink a few things on how I could get out there (figuratively speaking of course) while still maximizing my time. My goal was to spend the newly available down-time with safe, value added persons. And with a little luck, maybe even find a potential partner for dating on a reoccurring basis. Hence, I came up with a dry and sarcastic system that hopefully helps tremendously to deal with the stress of things. It may even provide a giggle or two along the way.

My mother would always say, '*If it's too good to be true, it probably is*' ... Sound familiar? Over time, my parents' words transformed into wisdom and I expanded those tips to other aspects of my life. You guessed it, dating. Maybe that's why I'm still single... hmmmm.

Alright, let's have some fun and think about

what you may want from dating in a pandemic. Yeah, I know, you want it all. Who doesn't, right? But it's a pandemic… perfection seeking isn't very realistic. Sadly, no one is perfect and that was Pre-COVID. Moving on, it sucks. Duh, I know, but bear with me. Here are some possible responses to that timeless question *'What do you want?' (Versus what is available out there)*.

- I want to stream movies with someone in safety, until this stupid pandemic is over.
- I *STILL* want the white picket fence family dream with someone. Yes, REALLY!
- I want someone to have fun with on weekends and GO OUT, even if it's takeout!
- I want a travel partner, even if traveling is limited.
- I want a dance partner on Saturday night, that's it. Yeah, and maybe some horizontal "*dancing*", too...

Having identified a few possible wants, we can take another step to further refine the *'want'*. This is key, as the main items of the *'want'* are built from internal desires and blown up by deal breakers. Remember realism here. It's all about managing one's expectations. Set the bar low and hopefully you will be pleasantly surprised. Let's expand on two of the samples from above:

- I want the white picket fence family dream with someone.
    - Who likes my children?
    - Who doesn't have more than 2+ children of their own?
    - Who must like my dogs, or better yet…? My dogs must like them.
    - Who is good at grilling, because I don't want to go out all the time?
    - Whose political affiliation needs to be at least close to mine…

- I want to stream movies with someone in safety
    - Who likes the same shows as I do?
    - Who has a similar schedule as I do?
    - Who is okay with talking on phone/facetime/whatever, while we watch?
    - Who *doesn't* talk during the show and interrupt the story line?
    - Who may be open to meeting in person, in the future, if I want to?

Alrighty, pull out your phone, notepad or whatever you need to create a list. It's the list of all lists. Begin to create the *'want'* list that applies to you. I know, you may think you can do this in your head but trust me. This fun activity of creating lists grows the more you read the guide. As you add items to the list, place a number of one to three importance to them (order doesn't matter). This way you can prioritize quickly. Using our example lists above:

- I want the white picket fence family dream with someone.
    - Who likes my children? **(1)**
    - Who doesn't have more than 2+ children of their own? **(2)**
    - Who must like my dogs, or better yet...? My dogs must like them **(1)**
    - Who can BBQ, I don't want to go out all the time? **(3)**
    - Whose political affiliation needs to be at least close to mine **(2)**

- I want to stream movies with someone in safety
    - Who likes the same shows as I do? **(2)**
    - Who has a similar schedule as I do? **(1)**
    - Who is ok with talking on phone/facetime/whatever, while we watch? **(2)**
    - Who *doesn't* talk during the show and interrupt the story line? **(3)**

- Who may be open to meeting in person in the future, if I want too? **(3)**

Ok, we're making progress. As I said before, this list may change and that's why we wrote it down. Don't be shy, list everything, even the bad stuff. So, how do you get what you want? Hard work? Well, I'm confident that I can safely say you have already tried that, otherwise why are you reading this guide? Back to the system I mentioned earlier. It's not magic, it's just data and, it's all about your list. Your list is how the system works. You know what you want, and what you're not going to deal with already, even in a pandemic. Now, let's jump into *'your'* system.

Note: If this is boring already, skip to the section titled 'We Actually do shit...'

Modus operandi

Hey, who doesn't love a good mystery where the bad guy has an Modus Operandi (M.O.), allowing the detective to capture them in the end? Well, depending on the perspective, the M.O. is helpful or a hinderance. Let's examine a sample M.O. and see where it leads. The dating scene is much like that favorite show, and it now offers a pandemic twist to the story line too. You and your soon to be significant other have an M.O. on how you find and select potential partners.

I recall thinking in the past that the office was more my home than where I slept. After all, I was there more than the place I paid for each month to keep my things at. I called it home, but was it? Working way too many hours in a large office, you get to know people and, in turn they get to know you. Late projects, weekend work or double shifts; this happens, that happens and next thing you know, you're either dating someone in the office or a family member of a coworker. That's awesome, and if the office is big enough you may be able to do that for a while and actually find someone. Unless it goes bad. Hmmm…new office, same behavior. Well shit, the pandemic just killed that because now we're all remote. Now WTF am I going to do? Thanks, COVID!

And here lies the problem; no office, limited bars, no gyms, and you guessed it… limited M.O. It's almost as if you're forced to do online dating. Or worse yet, the dreaded family/friend cupid… *'You and so-and-so would be perfect together'*. Eh, yeah that sucked Pre-COVID! …but maybe I could try that again…*<sigh>*

Transparency types

Yes, it's not just for the government, transparency is getting back to that realism we talked about previously. You know you have a type, but did you ever consider trying out a completely different type or finding a hybrid until this pandemic clears up? Yep, that sounds crazy I know but, what if? What if, you could mix and match types to that ideal perfection in your head, hmmm? Wake up, you're dreaming again… winning the lotto might be easier, but hey, somebody's gotta win eventually.

I listed some of the usual stereotypes below to help make you laugh and point out a few things. The goal is not to tell you what you already know but, to open your mind to other options as well as to the potential pitfalls for doing so. Who knows, it could be fun to experiment! COVID sucks, but perhaps you could use that as an excuse for trying out a new type?

Sports Nut

This one is self-explanatory, right? The person who is a wealth of information about sports. You name it and, they know it. Uh, yeah that was great before the pandemic... what now? People are shifting into other sports, moving away from the traditional sports your father might enjoy on television. The shift involves moving to MMA (mixed martial arts), car and motorcycling racing, X sports etc. You may be able to find something you can tolerate with the new categories and thus find a happy medium. At least it's not re-runs.

Bar Lounger

This type hasn't changed much over the years, but they sure are struggling during the pandemic when most bars are closed or seriously restricted. This also brings up the face mask issue depending on your feelings on the topic. They may be a good choice type, if they are ready for change depending on what features your looking for. More research will probably be required as waiting until closing to take someone home can be described as "*Hope is not a method (or strategy)*".

Home Body

The home body is usually a safe bet but is usually not that exciting. They may or may not have HGTV skills that include a few unfinished projects around the house. It's also possible that wild adventures are omitted from their upcoming calendar. Depending on what your *'want'* list entails, do not discount them. As we age, we tend to shift to a home body later in life anyways and remember it's a pandemic. You may get lucky, they could already be prepared and not going stir crazy.

News Junkie

They're either watching the stock market or switching between stations for all the current news feeds. This type needs constant data stimulation, with a limitless buffer overflow potential. Usually fast driven, type A peeps. Unfortunately, the news type may not be able to devote a significant amount of time for you. High stress based on the market indexes or news cycle may occur (*Doom Scrolling*). Refer to the drama factor section when considering this choice. Keep in mind they will always be tempted and/or captivated by the screen.

Computer Geek

The computer geek type may spend a considerable amount of time with computers and not notice that you have been sidelined. Geek time zones are not the equivalent time zones of most non geeks. This type requires time zone understanding along with isolation at varying times. If you're not familiar with geek time, it's similar to stoner time. Note that not all geeks are shy, lonely creatures locked away in mom's basement, even if in a pandemic.

The Gamer

The gamer, 'nough said. It might be fun at first to see them play games with your kids but, if they are playing games on the Xbox, Tablet or PC more than playing with you, it could be a problem in the future. Unless of course you're a gamer, too? Then hey, you have time in between map loads and/or respawns to get it on. Use caution or have fun as a new game is always coming out.

Comic-Con

The comic-con person is somewhere between gamer and traveling concert goer. They have a passion that is focused on everything about that one thing… If this isn't your cup of tea you may want to dig deep into understanding the category. In a pandemic, this person may be dressing up at home or attending zoom parties to get their fix. Which may be fun and even translate to some bedroom roleplay. Who doesn't want to re-enact Princess Leia and Han Solo getting it on?

Gun Pro

The gun aficionado is a shifting type, too. Gone are the days of hunting-only rifles. The reality is that many types of firearms are out there, and if you have some knowledge you can find common ground. Even though the gun ranges are closed, gun peeps still find places to exercise their firearms. Gun guys are always interested when a woman is gun friendly, knowledgeable, or enjoys guns. I mean how else can he say that cheesy line about helping you shoot his big gun... huh? And, uh, yeah, having a gun pro in the pandemic may not be all that bad.

Traveler

The traveler type has already been everywhere and has all the pictures to prove it. Their stories of travel are what other's dreams are made of. This can be a blessing or a curse depending on your list. If you want a travel guide, they could be the one. Who knows maybe all of those accumulated air miles will come in handy? That is after all the pandemic travel restrictions are lifted and you have a new vaccine approved passport <*Sigh*>. Get to know if they are open to re-tracing already traveled steps over the globe either in person, facetime or skype.

The Gym Rat

Yeah, you know this type. They spend a lot of time at the gym and they are all about the newest workout routine. But wow, do they look good. The downside - they know it. This type can be fun at first but, it's a lifestyle change if you are not the gym type. Diet restrictions, supplements, gym time requirements, etc. And not to mention the gym hot bod/bunny distractions. But this has changed in the pandemic. If they have yet to find workout equipment for the home gym, then most likely they have ventured out in search of a workout to get it done. Careful on this type, safety, or isolation sickness may be a factor. You may be able to shift the workouts to include you, two up yoga poses for Instagram, or perfecting your routine. Body shaping may be a new fun term that you can explore. Um, and you could get creative on the workout bench?

Drama factor

I'm sure we have all had the drama factor at a volume of ten at least once in a relationship. Some people thrive on it, while others dread it. Depending on where you rate yourself on the drama factor scale can help you further refine your list. A few things to keep in mind about the drama factor - drama has been proven to have an impact in every aspect of your wellbeing. If you have children or fur babies, they get the overflow of the drama, too. And now there's the added pandemic component. It has already added a significant amount of drama to our lives with just getting to the grocery store, buying toilet paper and other things. Now, add some relationship drama and yikes! If you think to yourself and say, "I despise drama!", I challenge you to look into the past. You may see some tell tales signs of Pre-COVID drama thriving. Drama thrives in the river of denial. Wait, no way! Are you sure? Here are some timeless examples of drama thriving:

- The sex was good, so I didn't mind the little things that really bothered me.
- They were so hot! I just ignored all the signs.
- I told their ex to stop calling... repeatedly.

- They didn't mean to do this or that.
- I had already spent so much time in developing the relationship, I just kept taking their shit.

Tell me who doesn't have at least some drama, right? This leads us into the drama factor and how it adds into your *'want'* list. We will use the drama factor as a multiplier in the system. Using a scale from 1 – 10, you simply select the drama factor amount you are willing to tolerate. The higher the number, the more drama you're okay with. Now, keep in mind that this is a subjective number. Number 1 is probably nonexistent in a pandemic, especially if you have children. Number 10 is best to avoid unless your only in it for the short term *(or if there's great sex, duh)*. So, as a starting point using a 5 or 6 as a good beginning number. We will get to how this is added into your list in the upcoming formula calculation section.

Story time. Yep, that's what we do in this guide. I share messed up stories that will hopefully make you laugh and that you may even be able to relate to a story from your own past. He we go…

Backyard family drama

It was summertime and I had been dating a girl for a while who really blew my socks off, if ya know what I mean. One typical weekend where heavy partying, "*wide-open throttle*" summed up the clothing optional activities where one could work up a sweat. I woke up early the morning after one such night filled activity thinking that coffee might help with my Texas-size headache. I yawned and put on my pants as she giggled in bed and rolled over to steal my pillow. As I began making the coffee in the kitchen, she called out asking me to add extra sugar to hers. I finished making the coffee and slowly turned around with both mugs in my hands. That's when I noticed a strange man in her backyard. I could see him though the large glass patio door. He was asleep, with his limbs outstretched wildly in the long uncut grass. Sunlight was beaming down on him like a heat lamp as he lay motionless. He appeared to either be homeless or maybe he had just escaped from jail. I paused looking intently for a moment while sizing him up. Suddenly, the girl interrupted my focus as she appeared before me wearing only my shirt. She must have noticed my laser focus pause because she gently grabbed a coffee from my hand, and as she did, she calmly whispered in my ear letting me know it was her brother. I was unsure how to react as I continued to stand there contemplating. She smiled and asked me if I wanted jump back into back to bed, while she strutted toward the bedroom showing off her assets. Of course, I should have run for the hills, the red flag drama alarm light was clearly at 1,000,000 lumens. Perhaps it was a lack of blood flow to my brain? I simply ignored that warning beacon along with that screaming voice in my head as I ran after her. Needless to say, that wasn't the last of the drama her brother offered, and it soon became overwhelming.

Note to self: family drama never goes away, it's like stepping in dog poop. It stinks and you tend to carry it with you everywhere you go. If you enjoy drama, feed off it, or otherwise can't avoid it, pick a high number.

Step: Calculate your drama factor and add it to your list.

1	2	3	4	5	6	7	8	9	10

Grey area of Liars and Ass Fuckery

Ah, to be young again and think everyone is always truthful and not just an asshole. Well, at over 40 I think we're past that now. Since we now know that quite a few people are liars and, in general, are hiding way too many things. We therefore need to be clever in our pursuit of happiness. Once again, I hear my mother and her many sayings *'Once a liar, always a liar'*. Normally, I would agree with her, but in some circumstances, you have a grey area. People will tell themselves lies all day, and then justify lying to anyone about even the silliest of things. This behavior is problematic as you can see. But one may allow a lie from their partner to slip by here and there, depending on the situation. For me, lying goes with secrets. They both suck! If you're looking for a lasting relationship of friendship, in my opinion, don't bother with consistent liars. Secrets never stay hidden, and they usually pop up at the worst possible time. I like to think of Mardi Gras on Bourbon Street - big parties, beer, beads, boobs, and massive fun, right? Then comes truth, it's like the monsoon rain washing away the party. The rain floods releasing the caskets filled with lies, secrets and skeletons for all the people you were hiding them from to see. Wow that's dark, huh? Not a good picture. Make it stop, *arrgghh!*

This is where the next category comes in, the grey area. The grey area consists of two main sub sections: Liars and Ass Fuckery. We already reviewed the liars but ass fuckery is a whole different quality. Ass fuckery can be simply defined as stupidity on a grand scale, with multiple levels. I like to use the term because it can easily encapsulate behavior patterns that should be reduced, or ideally extinct, when one reaches a certain age. Yeah, some might consider it to be the time you pretended to be a doctor for a night just to get someone into bed. But true Ass Fuckery mastery can go as far as messing with a persons' feelings, which is just plain wrong. I find it easier to add colorful stories when describing ass fuckery on a mastery level.

Ass Fuckery - Level: Master

I had met her online and she seemed to have it all together. I found this a tad bit suspicious, while researching her online presence. She was a ghost of sorts? I was unable to find out a lot about her. The first few dates went well but, I had this nagging feeling in the back of my mind. You know what I mean. Something was off, I just couldn't peg it. The relationship eventually progressed, and I chalked it up to my insecurities of her being too good for me, etc.

Our normal route of communication was through email and although I'm normally more of a phone person I went with it. It turns out that email was what ultimately revealed her secret. As I said, secrets never stay hidden. And when the incident originally happened, I thought to myself, *how did this happen?* You see, as I came to discover, she had an extra email account she used just to email me with. Her mistake came when at some point she added this additional account to her Outlook client. If you are unaware, you can have multiple email accounts linked in your Outlook client. Once she linked the two, the Outlook client inadvertently added a signature to her responses at which point I noticed that her last name was different. The last time I checked, people usually only change names with marriage. A little more digging on my part and, I found that she was, indeed, married. I felt bamboozled and let down. Was I just stupid, clueless, or was it that inner voice that I had ignored?

Even after discovering this, I decided to meet up with her to see what would happen. Could I catch her red-handed lying? Looking back, I guess I wanted an apology of sorts. How naïve of me. We met at a local pizza bar restaurant where we shared a meal. As the pizza arrived, I asked her how long she had been married. She didn't even hesitate to respond or deny it. In my continued state of bewilderment, I continued with my questions. Why hadn't she told me? How many other persons had she done this too before me? She claimed she had an open marriage and that he was aware. Then why keep it a secret? She had a response to all of my questions. She could lie like I had never witnessed before. No remorse and no feeling of wrongdoing whatsoever emitted from her sly silver tongue. It was when she asked how I knew that I got up from the table, placed a few dollars to cover my end of the tab and calmly walked out. I knew she had nothing else to offer and I kept the secret of devious discovery to myself. It made me feel at least a little better anyway.

There are levels of liars and degrees of practice in ass fuckery. Be cautious and listen to that inner voice. It's rarely wrong. I'm assuming you would rather avoid these shades of grey, so I recommend picking a low number here.

Step: Calculate your grey area and add it to your list.

1	2	3	4	5	6	7	8	9	10

Lost Art of Manners and the Wandering Eye of Shithead

Where to begin regarding manners. They are truly a lost art and, if you're trying to date a younger adult, they may even be considered passé. We could review the basics of being on time, putting your phone away during face-to-face conversations, or holding the door scenarios and the likes, but I think it may be related to common sense. If your *'want'* list requires manners from your partner, you may encounter a challenge in the area. I hear that there is a known deficiency of manners in the dating pool these days. Add a pandemic and the results are skewed further. We could spend endless pages on this topic, but why? You already know what you want.

Last, but not least, the Wandering Eye of Shithead. If you're into middle earth movies and the likes, you may understand the reference to the all-seeing eye. In the context of this book, it's about that person who just can't stop looking at everyone but you. This is annoying and shows a lack of respect, hence it fits right into the manner's category. This is a habit not easily corrected. Now, in all honesty, sneaking a peek every now and then is way different than what I'm referring to. Your ideal, long-term partner should only have eyes for you, especially when you're out on the town. This would include over-the-top ogling of online models, Facebook friends, thirst traps *(a sexy picture posted in the hope of gaining attention)*, naked screen savers, etc. If their eyes wander enough to where you notice it, then let's face it, they're a shithead.

Ok, lets jump into a good story, one which I truly couldn't make up if I tried. Yes, it's from pre-COVID, but all the good stories are...so far.

Manners, the lack thereof...

The girl was stunning, and I was captivated by her presence. We laughed during our good conversations and the few dates we had gone on always seemed to run over the normal time newly met strangers typically spend together. During this particular date, we were at a sea food restaurant and it was quite enjoyable. In bliss I intently watched her in her sunflower dress as she smiled back at me from across the table. Our meal had been served and we casually ate while exchanging flirtatious comments about upcoming deserts. The waiter cleared the table and had just left to retrieve the dessert menu when it happened. I wish I could have seen my reaction at the time. This beautiful girl had quickly turned her head to the side, her long brown hair flowing as she did, but as I continued to watch her, oddly her hand grabbed her mouth and she inserted her fingers. In less than a second, and without warning, she pulled out a large portion of her teeth with a light snapping noise. And with that, she placed them into her drinking water glass on the table! She then began swishing them about, removing the food particles that had become lodged over the course of the meal. Without hesitation, she slid them back into her mouth and started our conversation back up as if nothing had transpired. Now, I like to imagine that I did my best to keep a straight face, but I can never be sure if I succeeded in that or not. As I watched the food floaties in her drinking water sink toward the bottom of the glass, I was dumb founded. Not by her lack of teeth, but by her manners for pulling them out and washing them in her drinking water glass. I had never encountered that type of behavior in a restaurant before and I was unsure on how best to react. I wondered to myself, was it just her way to get that information out on the table (*figuratively speaking of course, but...well, kind of literally, too, in this case, I guess*) or was this action something else.

In this situation, I had learned something about myself as well. I did have an expectation or level of manners that I wanted from my potential dates. I did try to get past this incident with this girl, but unfortunately in the end, this behavior was the norm in other areas as well. After this discovery, you can surmise it just didn't work out. If you have spent considerable time with partners in the past in regard to manners, this may not be a big deal but it's a personal choice. Perhaps a middle number will work out if you're in doubt. Afterall, if they were perfect, they likely wouldn't be single right?

> Step: Calculate your Manner's factor and add it to your list.

1	2	3	4	5	6	7	8	9	10

Health

It's a survival guide in a pandemic, so of course there is a health section. And everyone has health issues. No, I'm not overstating the obvious. What I'm doing is slapping you in the face with some super real facts. Cancer survivor, automotive accident, diabetes, or prosthetics are not usually noticeable when first meeting people. Health is a huge factor in any relationship whether you want to acknowledge it or not. The pandemic adds gasoline to this fire by making it difficult to go to the doctor. I mean do you really want to go where people are sick right now? In all seriousness, people have avoided the dentist, the doctor in general and OMG the hospital as much as possible. This has left many health issues undiagnosed and/or untreated. This is problematic and most likely will impact you at some point.

It's all in your head

This area can be controversial, which means ya know we gotta talk about it. It's mental health and it's a thing as you know. Now, I'm not talking about your mentally unstable serial killer or shit like that. I'm talking about the more common, but less talked about, afflictions that most of the population actually experience. Not all mental illnesses are the same and there is a wide range of how they impact individuals. Here is a story that highlights just one example.

I had met her online, she stood out with a great profile *(just enough words with good pictures, including a full body shot)*. She was sassy and exhibited a strong personality. She held a job of prominence in government and I found her company very enjoyable. We had been dating awhile and it was quite nice. We were at the stage of getting to know more about her family when it went sideways. Oftentimes getting family information can be challenging but she was especially secretive, and it was a red flag for me. I brought this up with her and mentioned she was not acting like herself. I had not seen her act this way about other topics and I was taken aback by her behavior. This went on and off for a week until she stopped by my place out of the blue. She had been crying and claimed she needed to tell me something. In my head I panicked and thought the worst.

She was seated on my couch with tears running down her face as she continued. She explained that she had a family history of mental illness and that she, in fact, had a mental disorder herself. She preferred not to discuss it just yet but informed me that she was going in for treatment the next day for. She would be recovering for a few days and then she would tell me everything. I reassured her that things were okay between us and that I would wait for her to explain things when she was ready. She thanked me for my understanding and left for the evening. It was about a week later that she called and wanted to go to dinner. I agreed and we met up. It was rather awkward at first, as she struggled to recall certain memories, and then she just blurted it out in frustration. She was getting electroconvulsive therapy (*ECT*) treatment and it was impacting her memory. She wasn't sure if she wanted to continue dating due to her treatment, but she was conflicted about it. I was at a total loss as she continued telling me about her treatment, including that it could continue for some time. Our dinner was her way of explaining to me that she had issues and that she needed time to deal with them. I really respected her for taking the time to explain it to me in person. After dinner, she kissed me goodbye and I never saw her again. I learned so much that night but yet I knew there was so much more that I didn't know.

As I mentioned, everyone has health issues. Some of them are physical and others are mentally based. Being comfortable in speaking about them with your potential partner is big but, knowing what you and your partner may be taking on in a relationship is huge.

Note: Mental illness is not a joke and I mean to bring awareness with this story as well as highlight its common place. If you are unsure about your mental stability, please seek professional help without shame or embarrassment.

> **The NAMI Help Line can be reached Monday through Friday, 10 am–6 pm, ET.**
> 1-800-950-NAMI (6264) or info@nami.org

Exercise, do something…

Holiday pounds, baby weight, love handles, spare tire… you know the terms. The never-ending battle where the older we get, the harder it is to maintain a healthy lifestyle and/or shape. Do not despair, it happens to the best of us. How couldn't it not with work, kids, stress, mid-life crisis, right? The stress from a pandemic doesn't help either. I sometimes find myself stress eating over this doom and gloom shit show. This crosses over into our dating life too, not because we have a few extra pounds but because a poor diet impacts our motivation. Finding a partner to help maintain or start working on positive motivation is a great option. Maybe you can add this to your *'want'* list.

I know what you're thinking, *"Uh, you make it sound easy. How can I incorporate exercise into my daily routine?"* I used to think that walking was for old people *(shit, I'm old now)* until I started doing it.

It was a wakeup call for me. I would consider myself in decent shape but there is always room for improvement. I often sit for far too long during the work day and so, to break up that time, I tried walking. I was surprised at how far I *couldn't* walk. Each week I tried to add 10-15 feet on to my walk until I could make it around the block. After a month or so I was actually getting to enjoy it. I could hear the birds chirp, and admire the green trees and blue sky, plus I was beginning to trim up a bit. It did wonders for my motivation just being outside and that helped in a lot of other areas including dating.

Perhaps you could walk the mall or local park with a date during the pandemic. It's easy to stay socially distanced and maybe you can even find humor together while trying to have conversation with your masks on. Either way just keep this in the back of your mind - peeps that do things together, stay together. Oh, and yep, sex is great exercise, too (*although a bit more difficult with a mask on!*).

Napping can be fun!

Okay, I realize I'm doing a 180 on you here, jumping from exercise to sleeping, but bear with me. Afternoon naps are not just for the children anymore. I recall it seemed like yesterday when I could drink Red Bull and stay up all night. I would casually stroll into to work drinking a gallon of coffee if I felt a tad bit tired the next morning. Well, those days are long gone, and now I hear that caffeine calling me just in order to get to work after sleeping most of the night. This brings up an important aspect of your life that you should consider when dating. Your sleep time! Sleeping has numerous health benefits as I'm sure you already know, but just like with our cell phones, that battery inside of us doesn't recharge as fast as it used to. Have you ever tried taking a cat nap? I personally love them and if we had a couch at work, I would consider napping at lunch instead of eating. If you don't believe me, just try it. Practice taking a fifteen-minute nap on a Saturday, mid-day, to get your bearings. You may find it a refreshing break. Setting aside time for a recharge is similar to meditation. It can do wonders for your mind, body and health.

Please keep in mind some people may have health concerns regarding sleep *(such as sleep apnea, snoring which may require a CPAP machine)* as they age, so be aware.

Note: Did you know that as we age the potential to snore increases as well as how volume of our snoring… Ah, the many gifts of aging.

If this could be a factor for you, be upfront and talk about it. You and your partner will find out eventually, especially if they are sleeping next to you. Ask about it in a silly way, perhaps a snoring challenge to lighten things up a bit.

Up, Down and out

Let's tie this all together with another fun story. I had landed a new job and it was quite challenging. I found balancing work, home and family getting more difficult as the time went by. It was a slow process at first, but I soon found myself drinking multiple cups of coffee to keep up. This in turn grew to even more coffee consumption, followed by soda, energy drinks, etc. My sleep cycle was all out of sync due to the caffeine in my veins and the emails dinging from my phone. I had little time to cook any food for my lunch, which led to a fast-food diet that spiraled its way into my dating life. My girlfriend at the time was kind enough to point out that my job was not healthy and that if I didn't change course soon, I would be navigating alone. I believe it was when I had fallen asleep at my girlfriend's house for the third time on a date night that she finally let me go…

Vitamins, caffeine and prescription drugs, along with fast food can all have an impact on a person's health, which ultimately transforms into long term behaviors that may or may not be healthy in a relationship. Try to weigh their use in your mind and know your limits.

The overall health of a short-term partner may not be as impactful as for an intended long-term partner, but still use caution. Some short-term partners can sometimes end up becoming long term ones *(Especially in a pandemic)*. Ask questions and make sure you are comfortable with your partner's potential health concerns. Try to be empathetic and honest as you may have to share your health issues as well. And for goodness sake keep in mind that due to this lovely pandemic some health concerns are yet to be discovered. If your partner's health is a big concern, up the number that you pick below.

Step: Calculate your Health factor and add it to your list.

1	2	3	4	5	6	7	8	9	10

Vegas Baby

I loved Vegas when I was younger! It really was the city that never slept. During my younger years, I was guilty of practicing Ass Fuckery whenever I was there, but today the pandemic has changed Vegas. It has been morphed into something trendier now with COVID plastic walls and shields in place everywhere...how *vogue*! Still, it offers a compact all-inclusive fun trip in multiple areas. Why do I bring Vegas up? Because it's a great way to get more information about a potential partner's current behavior patterns. Past and present behaviors can help you direct your line of questioning to your '*want*' list. And pre-COVID behaviors are easy tell tales to the behaviors of current and post-COVID ones.

Who doesn't have a Vegas story? It's possible that some don't, but a majority of us have at least one (and some of us significantly more than one). You may have heard those silly sayings related to "*when you're in different zip codes*" and such, that can often be tied to Ass Fuckery. My point is, you want to find out, did your significant other get all of that crazy out of their system already? When I get asked about Vegas, I share the story about the time when a friend and I flew into

Vegas and never got a hotel room. We called it the *'Iron-Man'*. It was a non-stop party until we flew home. We had a rule that all of the money we won, we had to spend while there. Limos, shows, rides, expensive dinners, you name it *(yes, strippers)*, we did it. Yes, I did all of that... But it was over twenty years ago. I wouldn't even dream of doing it now, with or without an on-going pandemic. Which brings me to a big topic of this section, gambling. Everyone is different, and gambling can be fun, but sometimes it can be a problem.

My friend's sister is very smart. She had a great job and it seemed that everywhere she went, great things happened to her. Eventually she met an all-American athletic type stud and turned it into the type of relationship they base Hallmark movies on. I mean it almost made me puke up into my nose. Yeah, that kind of relationship. They were was bliss in the making...until his gambling addiction blew it all up. I mean, <u>*blew it up*</u>! I recall thinking *where did that come from*? Were there warning signs she overlooked? Or was it something that he just lost control of? I never did find out for sure, but it instilled me with the *'be on the lookout for this behavior'*.

Now, don't think that gambling is a buzzkill for goodness sake. It's not. I mean, I love yanking slots, blackjacking cards, and most of all, rolling dice at the craps table as much as the next guy. My preferred Vegas scene, you ask? Free drinks, no clocks, and a group of my drunken friends with me while lady luck blows on my dice. Now we're talking fun! And that's before we go to a show with an erotic theme. *(No, that's not my grown-up way of saying the strip club. Vegas offers a wide variety of shows where performers really do some amazing things.)* This is the Vegas I love and remember.

Getting back to the "Vegas, Baby" Factor. I view it as the ability to get buck wild before and/or after establishing a relationship. If you still need to go a little crazy from time to time, increase your number. I would use a three if you have slowed down a bit, but can get wild if needed on occasion. If you're the "ALL Vegas Baby", and you need to party hard because you missed out earlier in life, then yes, 11 is available.

Caution: I don't believe in the saying, *"What happen in Vegas, stays in Vegas."* Highly unlikely… secrets don't stay secrets when X marks that spot.

Step: Calculate your Vegas Baby and add it to your list.

1	2	3	4	5	6	7	8	9	10	11

Hot Mess Factor

You may or may not be familiar with this term. A better question is why is it in this guide? Well, it's pretty simple, in fact. Because let's face it, you have probably met someone, or have been a hot mess yourself, at least once in your life by now. Before we get started on this section, we need to review the term. Merriam-Websters Dictionary defines it as one of two main terms. The first being about food but that's not our focus here. The second one is… you guessed it… about something (*ha, someone*) that is in extreme disarray or disorder with the added level of being self-destructive, while at the same time still being considered hot and physically desirable. Although the term can be considered derogatory in the wrong circumstances, it's my opinion that most people see it as positive description with a twist. The twist sometimes referring to the potential for crazy hot sex.

Yeah ok, but how does this factor into a pandemic? Well, add stress, children, job, vaccines, lack of getting out and dating etc. and you can easily resemble/become a hot mess. We could dive into the hot vs. crazy sex equation, but a video already exists on YouTube that details the correlation of hot and crazy, including the unicorn theory, so you can go check it out for yourself. Either way, the Hot Mess Factor differentiates from the Vegas section in that it highlights you don't need to travel in order to get your freak on. Even if you're a temporary pandemic hot mess or you're looking for one due to certain unfulfilled needs it's a factor. Hey, no judgment here. If you need or want more in the area of sexual pleasure/arousal on a regular basis then you need to up your calculation for the '*Hot Mess Factor*' scale.

Too '*Hot*' for me…

Alright, story time again. I was a younger man at the time, working in an office doing the day-to-day thing, when I met her. She was quite a looker and I wasn't the only one who would get caught peeking at her when she sauntered by. She was a bit older than me, but I was drawn to her alure. She was a hot mess and I knew it. Sloppy but sexy in the way she dressed and her attitude was dangerous. So, of course, I found out everything I could about her from the office gossip pool. All of this data only made me more interested in her, but looking back, I felt she was out of my league. I guess she heard about my inquiries about her so one day she surprised me in the hallway. She was definitely not shy and asked me point blank when I had planned on asking her out. I probably turned bright red as I stuttered back in response. Well, as you can imagine our dating whirlwind went 100 miles per hour with her at the wheel driving like a bat out of hell. She literally wore me out with sex, much to my surprise. Her freak level was one I had not experienced before, nor could have predicted. I wasn't complaining, mind you, but I was beginning to think things might be getting out of hand. Sure, banging in the parking lot during lunch was fun but, the volume only went louder from that point on. You name it, we did it, with no end in sight. I found myself not wanting to ride that edge of being an exhibitionist or diving into some bizarre whips and chains shit. That's when the bottom dropped out of the relationship. It was a total reversal from my previous relationships. I was now the one saying slow down, hold up, let's pace ourselves. Which then eventually turned into me getting dumped. Needless to say, that job didn't work out long after that either.

This point in time helped me understand what my comfort level (*freak level*) was and how I wanted my partner to be in a similar way. Kinda like finding the Goldilocks zone – not too much, not too little, but just right! As we all know, *'No freak is equal. They are separated by varying degrees.'* Finding the right fit in your range is key to the Hot Mess Factor. So, using the scale of 1-10 if you want more freak, pick a higher number.

Step: Calculate your Hot Mess factor and add it to your list.

Hygiene Anyone

I guess this is a strange topic in a dating guide, but we should review. I think you may have guessed that I'm not talking about if your partner likes facial hair or perhaps doesn't shave under their arms. We should agree that in a pandemic certain hygiene habits may fall to the side with high stress levels or working remotely for months. This could include patchy unkept beards, leg shaving strikes, or every day is a ponytail day with no make-up. This hygiene section dives into the messed-up way people view hygiene. I'm guessing you may have, at some point in the past, met that special person and were taken aback by how obtuse they were in regard to personal hygiene. Hey, we all sweat and, yeah, at over 40 you may have a few dental concerns, too. This is normal stuff, but hopefully our hygiene has improved from our younger self, and we still maintain it to a certain level, even in a pandemic.

With that said, how do you talk about the awkwardness of hygiene with a potential or current partner? Well, shit howdy, I'm clueless, too! What I can tell you is that it's better to express your preferences upfront than to be taken aback with surprises. What? Laymen terms please!

Ok, here are some lovely examples. Wearing so much cologne/perfume that others become almost nauseous within a 6-foot social distance area *(Not good)*. Too much makeup that people may not recognize what your skin really looks like underneath, let alone under that cloth face mask. Oh, and here is a good one… If you prefer a reduced or shaved pubic region, speak up and say so! Cause let's be real, when you're in happy-go-mode and WHAM that tangled jungle surprise jumps out, uh, that may take the wind out of those sails. Really? Yep. How about decayed teeth, bad breath action, or nasty snot snorting. Do those items need mentioning too?

Hygiene Deuce

You guessed it, story time. In this section, I have two stories. Bonus! The first one is some advice I gave a friend of mine. He was dating and he had asked for feedback on why he wasn't having any luck with the ladies. (Ha ha, yeah, *'asking for a friend'* comes to mind here but, in this case, it truly happened.) Anyway, if you're like me, you do your best when friends ask for advice and you try to be polite, at least at first. But this was something that my friend just wouldn't let go. After trying the polite route at first, I finally let him have it. I asked him to look in the mirror and smile. As he did, I asked him if he knew what plaque was and I threw in some info about the potentially harmful effects to his overall health. My friend froze, mortified by his reflection. He saw it clearly then. I continued on by suggesting breath mints to improve his breath, which led to him telling me off as he stormed out of the room. You see, my friend hadn't been to the dentist in quite some time and the plaque buildup between his teeth was long overdue for a cleaning and was impacting his breath in a very negative way. As if struck with lightning purpose, my friend soon scheduled a dentist appointment, and shortly after his dating prospects began to increase. Now, whether that was from better dental hygiene or confidence, I couldn't tell you.

Ok, the second story is mine alone. Yep, I had met a new girl and we had been on a few dates. We had gone out for drinks and light dancing and the night was going well. We got a bit tipsy as the night progressed and one thing led to another. We found ourselves in the car steaming up the windows in the parking lot. She was ready to go when the incident caught me off guard. It sidetracked the moment, not because of the facts, but the location and timing. As she took off her pants and jumped on my lap, I felt a string brush my leg. I interrupted our make out session to ask her, "Is that a tampon string?"

Without hesitation she responded, "Oops, I got it…"

I didn't understand what she meant until she quickly pulled her tampon out, showing little concern. As the tampon fell to the car floorboard, I wasn't thinking that was the problem. It was the heavy flow that followed right behind it onto my lap that caught my complete attention. Ewww!

Here's the thing, if hygiene is important for you then try emphasizing that, but I hope you are acting accordingly. If you are actually trying to make a good impression, then be presentable and considerate. Duh. And be upfront. Here are some fun ways to communicate and be playful while doing so, especially in a pandemic where norms are now not so black and white.

- "Just so you know, I like going below the equator if the jungle isn't overgrown."

- "I'm ok with period sex, but perhaps we can practice in the shower."

As for the calculation, hygiene can usually be sorted out between couples with communication. A higher number indicates you're ok with unkept hygiene and unsanitary norms. Who knows? That might be your thing.

Step: Calculate your *'Hygiene Anyone'* and add it to your list.

Financial Savvy

Being financially savvy is a foundational skill set for a long-term relationship but not so much for a short term one, regardless of pandemic status. If you are in it for the short term, you can most likely skip this shit. Your only concern is that your date shows up and possibly pays for the date as needed. Long-termers, hold fast and keep reading.

If you were unaware, financial problems contribute to a majority of relationship failures. Clearly money, or more often the lack of it, creates a stress inducing phenomenon. Knowing in advance how stable a potential long-term partner is, the better prepared you will be. Yep, I know you didn't forget about the pandemic causing massive unemployment and housing concerns. This could be a huge lead up into financial stability. Hey, shit happens. Being upfront and honest about it usually doesn't. Making a plan to fix it is even more uncommon.

I'd Gladly Pay You Tuesday…

A quick story from a female friend of mine. It's one of those stories that was just so lame from a guy's perspective that I just never forgot it. Okay, imagine this gal is having dinner with this guy at a nice but not too upscale restaurant. He had been chasing her for quite some time masquerading as a well to do gentlemen. He had finally worn her down overtime to get his chance with her on a dinner date. You would think that he would have all the bases covered at this point, after trying so hard for so long. Either way, as my friend tells it, the dinner was going well and the conversation wasn't inadequate. She even mentioned that she stayed for dessert. Her reasoning was that she was unsure on reading this guy. He was somewhat charming and mysterious in a way, I guess. That would have been my first red flag.

News Flash: You're over 40 and if you can't read someone. It may be because they are hiding shit about who they really are *(Ass Fuckery)*, or you have just woken up from a coma. Use caution, trust your gut.

Moving on. They wrap up dinner as she unfolds the story further telling me that this guy may actually have a chance to get to round two. This is when the shit hits the fan. The check comes and the guys exclaims with bravado confidence that he will cover it. My friend sat back playing her part, allowing him this moment of gusto. But if you recall, he did ask her out. **The guy handbook clearly states: if you ask, you pay. Unless otherwise noted.** The waitress takes his card and as she heads to her work station, the guy then proceeds to hint to my friend about "round two", among other things. At this point my friend is mildly amused at his boyish attempts... until the server comes back. The waitress presents his card along with the unfortunate news that it was declined. Uh, hard stop. What happened? Yes, a crack appears in the charming fellow façade as he fumbles to pull out another card. His chances of getting to round two begin to lose altitude rapidly. *'Cue airplane nose-dive sound now...'*

And yes, you guessed it, the waitress returns yet again with another declined card. At this point the airplane nose-dive crash sound erupts into a savage explosion. What does my friend do? I applauded her behavior and thought what a class act as she described the ending. She calmly pulled out her purse, silently passed her credit card to the waitress while this guy profusely apologized. The waitress came back in record time knowing my friend was in a dire situation. My friend tipped the waitress well and then proceeded to ask the loser with her (*her date*) if he wanted a drink from the bar. Both the waitress and her date looked a bit confused but he must have seen it as a chance for him to explain the situation in detail. My friend politely got up from the table and motioned him towards the bar area of the restaurant as she headed toward the lady's room. When she was out of eyesight, she told me that she left the restaurant. I asked her, why did you ask him if he wanted a drink? Two reasons, she said. One was that he clearly needed to put out the flames of crashing and he may meet someone new at the bar. The second, it allowed her to make a strategic retreat without the added drama. As I admired her cleverness, I asked how would he pay if his cards were declined? She chuckled a bit, simply stating that she surmised he did have some cash on him. Enough for a few drinks anyways, along with a ride home.

It made me think that must have happened before to her or someone she knew. I also thought that she was probably right about him having enough for drinks and a ride. It reminded me of a few of my old drinking buddies that needed me to buy them beer inside the bar but always seemed to have money for food at the afterhours place. After hearing that story, I always carried backup cash when taking someone out. I never wanted to be the main character of a story like that.

Financial Shit Heads

Have you ever started dating what seemed like a good choice for a partner when all of a sudden, they morphed into a penniless mooch? Well, you are not alone. There isn't any sure-fire way to spot a scammer *(a good one anyways)*, but they often present themselves with small red flags. Be on the lookout for behavior tells that may not match what they may have communicated in a profile. Some of the telling signs include, they ask a lot of favors that aren't returned, convincing you to pay for things that you normally wouldn't, not contributing their share, helping themselves to your items in general, leaning toward ass fuckery and/or playing the victim card. You can try and fix a mooch but then again, why? Shit can them and move on!

How about the great catch that has shitty credit or is massively deep in debt? Well, shit howdy again, right? This is a concern but its more about digging deep to find a root cause. Divorce can wreak havoc on finances as well other sensitive topics. Oh yeah, hello pandemic…Knowing this, don't overlook the pitfall of not having the hard talk about understanding. You will want to know eventually anyways, so why wait? Rip that band-aid off ASAP. If the reasoning is sound, and they are open to discussing a plan of action for recovery, then make a judgement call. If your gut sends up the bullshit card, 86 their ass. *(86, is the old term slang for getting rid of things, similar to file 13)*

Red flags for financial impending doom:

- Seeing a stack of bills/final notice indicators at your partner's place.
- A purse or wallet filled with numerous credit cards.
- Uncontrolled shopping habits, frivolous spending unchecked.
- A lot of your dates are based on shopping/buying opportunities.
- Ignorant of high interest rates or a big believer in buy now pay later.

- Lying about the cost of things to hide ineptitude of being financial savvy.
- Their standard of living is, or seems, higher than what (you assume) their income/employment would allow for…

Using some of the techniques in the *'We actually do shit'* section that's coming up can help you evaluate the situation, but when in doubt, again, trust your gut.

Here is another scenario I hear about more often than you would think. You may have experienced it. The smart investor and the once in a lifetime opportunity. It always reminds me of a country song with ocean front property for sale in Arizona. In my experience, the story usually starts with a whirlwind romance, followed up by chance encounter of a family member or long-lost friend. Upon this chance encounter your special person mentions this opportunity for an (insert - money, gold, art, business, stocks, livestock, cryptocurrency) awesome deal. And just because you're dating or know '*so and so*' you, too, can take part in said opportunity. Or better yet, they had a rich uncle die and they have half of the money to invest but need your help. If this happens, you'd better double check your shit. This is another reason why you only give out information about yourself and your financial situation in small increments until you have established a good foundation.

Wait, this is a movie, right? Alas, <*sigh*> I want to say if it is, you are playing the mark role. The one who gets taken. How do you think they get the ideas to write those movies? By making shit up or from real life scenarios? It happens. Be on the lookout for something too good to be true. Times are tight, especially during a pandemic, and although you may not think you are rich, you are likely doing a lot better than some people out there. And you want something, which makes you vulnerable. What do I want? Duh, love…*(or a version of it).* If you are still not convinced that bad actors like this are out there, I have one word for you. Catfishing.

So, when calculating your financially savvy person, aim low. Meaning you don't want a lot of bullshit with financial matters because *'hello'* life is hard enough. Three is a good starting number because everyone has some sort of shit going on.

Step: Calculate your 'Financial Savvy' and add it to your list.

1	2	3	4	5	6	7	8	9	10

Personality test / S.T.A.R

The personality test approach can be useful to help find that special someone. Depending on your *'want'* list this may seem like overkill, but there have been proven studies that indicate certain personalities couple better. It also helps understand some questions that may help determine if the person you are interested in is truly a match. (*I'm assuming long term relationship here. Short term hookups... this may help you get to the specifics of the bump and grind you desire*). It also helps to know yourself before attempting to know others. A popular personality test is the Myers Briggs. To find out more about the personality types they list, simply use your search engine and read more about it. Hey, it's free... have you taken it yet?

The last time I went for a job interview, I researched the STAR method of answering questions. If you're not familiar with the STAR method, it's an acronym - (S) situation, (T) task, (A) action, and (R) result. Uh, but this is dating not a job interview. You could say that but aren't they really the same thing? Both are a conversation / dialog based on a list of requirements. And the STAR method is a great technique to use for any communication. It helps get data needed in assessing your *'want'* list. It can offer a lot more than just one word or short answers.   Just like during an interview with an employer, when on a date you are looking for someone based on a list of wants/needs and the other person is responding by saying they meet those requirements. During this conversation, each party asks questions and decides if the other person is a good fit. Usually, you are thinking about the benefits of a good "*fit*" during an interview. After all, that's why you applied, isn't it?

The new employee

One could debate the many similarities that exist between a new employee and a new dating partner. It could be its own a comedic standup skit. The comic could start with…

"…Ya know, my last significant other… wow. It reminded me of the new person at the office. They did great in the interview; dressed for success, sharp as a tack, met the requirements and the attitude was outstanding. A few weeks on the job and they called out sick. No worries, I thought to myself, it happens. It was still going well! Then a few more weeks later, the work they output started to become sub-standard. Hmmm, this was when I became concerned. It was right about at that 90-day mark where I had to consider whether to keep them on the payroll… I thought back to the interview and asked myself, did we check references? It became clear that more in-depth questions were missed when HR asked why the police were here talking with them. "

With this silly story in mind, perhaps the STAR method could help you when you're having a conversation with a potential date. I try to use open-ended questions, but clearly you need to tweak them a bit to fit the dating scenario, otherwise, they **DO** sound like job interview questions. Consult your favorite search engine for open-ended dating questions and see what you can improvise using the STAR technique. Oh, and don't forget to take those mental notes for later. How else are you going to keep track of who said what…

Hey if this seems lame my Mom would say *'Don't knock it, 'til ya tried it! You may be surprised as hell.'*

PADTFM, Oh My

Politics, Alcohol, Drugs, Tobacco, Firearms and Masks, oh my. Yep, these are usually the high-ranking questions in the red flags section, labeled as deal breakers to most. Drugs kind of fall into that grey area regardless of a pandemic. Questions around drug use, even if mild, can transform into a colorful past and/or future incarceration concern. If you have that perfect partner on the line and you're in doubt, ask yourself what your comfort level is.

Politics

Well, yikes, is all I can say. The pandemic didn't help this area one bit with things like beliefs regarding governmental lockdown orders, opinions regarding restaurant take-out, viewpoints surrounding face masks, etc. Politics has become quite a category when dating. I would recommend getting the politics out in the open and see what happens. Some people are passionate about it, while others are more middle of the road types. Either way this could be a huge (*Bigly*) dealbreaker for you...

Alcohol

Yeah, it's a topic that can have its own book. I'll try to sum it up like politics - moderation is the key. Outside of that it can be tricky with an ongoing pandemic as sometimes judgement can fall out the window or too much consumption can occur. It's 5'oclock somewhere can lose its luster quite rapidly.

Tobacco

It's not a secret why those cool warning labels are affixed to the boxes. It's a health concern, but especially during a pandemic that has an impact on the respiratory system. This could be a deal breaker to some, or a chance to quit for others. I have yet to see a mask that allows for smoking tobacco, but maybe it's too soon?

Firearms

This is a huge category that I'm going to attempt to tap dance around because there is such a wide array of beliefs, concerns and so many overall choices. Depending on your *'want'* list and your safety concerns, when it comes to you and your partner, ask away. The silver lining of gun ownership in a pandemic is safety. Some might say it's better to have one and not need it, than to need one and not have it. I'll let you decide…

Face Masks

Pandemic safety gear *(This includes vaccines, too)*. Some may equate this to reefer madness *(Pot induced lunacy)*, others may be donning a full hazmat suit to check the mail. Either way, you will have to decide what works for you, and what you are willing to deal with from a potential partner. Because let's face it, if you can't agree on this then how are you going to overcome social distancing and get it on?

Using your cunning skills, get more data on these particular items by asking bold questions, with a sly tact. I like to use the technique of storytelling to lure out the data and then follow up with bold questions. Now, keep in mind your *'want'* list may not require you to get this data, but then again it might.

Pandemic Party Story

I was talking to a friend of mine who was planning a party during the middle of the pandemic. She was persistent on getting me to RSVP for the event happening in her backyard. I was hesitant because I didn't know how many people would be attending and, duh, the pandemic! She kept saying, *"Hello, single ladies, come on!"* I heard myself mumbling my response with a blah, blah, yeah, okay. She was over the moon and let me know that twenty or so people would be over for the event. I was dreading the day as it quickly approached. I remember driving over to her house and entering the backyard with a face mask on, not knowing what to expect. I felt so out of place; I was the only one wearing a mask. I tried to fit in, and she teased me until I removed it. I did my best to social distance, but it was worse than Pre-COVID parties I had attended. It was a party alright and, I was missing out. How do you mingle with strangers in a pandemic? How do you get close and start up a conversation while social distancing? I ended up leaving early, feeling silly for attending in the first place.

Why is this story relevant in this section? It's a reminder to be okay with what *you* want. It's a pandemic and personal safety is unique to us all. Your mask preferences are the same as all of you other **PADTF** preferences. You need to decide ahead of time what you're okay with and don't be swayed by others who may not share those same preferences.

STI -STD – WTF

Sexual transmitted infections/diseases are gifts that no one really wants, ones that you can't return, and the gifts that usually keep on giving. Awkward topic? Yes. It can be even worse in a pandemic where people are not going to the doctor as much. Assuming you're into a person and you think you may be willing to jump on, STI/STD should be a focus point, right? But how do you get this out there? Yeah, I know… WTF. If you have an STI/STD be upfront about it. Communication is key. You may be surprised by your new interest's response.

If you are interested in more current statistical data, search for *'CDC std stats'* in your favorite search engine. And HIV is still a very real concern. Once again search *'HIV data trends HIV.gov'* you may be surprised at the data presented.

Note: The term 'Super gonorrhea' is now all the rage. I don't know why super makes it any worse. If anything, you should be hyper vigilant.

If you are STI/STD free *(ya' don't have any)* and not sure how to ask a potential partner what their status is, just be honest. I've just always used the straightforward approach, explaining that I practice safe sex. Seems simple enough and it usually confirms that, if they somewhat agree, intimacy could occur in the future. After I get the green light on that, I bluntly ask. "*Do you have any STI-STD's?*"

Yes, at times you may get an awkward silence or bewildered look. But hang in there; remember you would prefer to remain STI/STD free, correct? Now, if you get a 'Yes' response, well, that's for you to decide on what to do next. But consider your options and <u>be kind.</u> They did just reveal very personal, private information, and you should admire them for their honesty. If you get a 'No', here is the follow up question you can use that most people would not expect. "I always get a STI/STD test from my doctor and share it with my partner before intimacy. Would you be willing to do that?"

That may seem too bold but what you are asking is protecting you and them. A lot of people do not know that they have been exposed. Up-to-date testing is for everyone's safety. It could help you, them or others in the future. Don't feel bad about it. This is even more paramount in a pandemic. Upfront and honest health conversations are important factors to building trust and a lasting relationship *(or short intense fuck fests)*. Regardless of which way you're going, be safe when getting together.

STI –STD Awareness

I'll share a Pre-COVID story that really brings this topic home. I was with my doctor one day and she asked if I was still single. I responded jokingly asking her, what would her husband say? She returned my sarcasm with a disapproving look and indicated that she wasn't asking on her own behalf, but on behalf of another patient of hers that she had been treating. First, I thought wow HIPPA Anyone. But she claimed she was asking in an anonymous way. If I agreed, it would truly be a blind date. My doctor could share nothing…I would have to fully rely on her judgement. I thought, why not, right?

I agreed to a blind date with this new girl and we met at a local sushi restaurant after a short phone conversation. She was very pleasant and we had good conversation over a light meal. We went out a few times after that and things were going quite well. It was time for the question. You know the STI/STD question. She had responded *'No'* and I went on to the next question about getting a test from the doctor and providing the results. She agreed and I went to the doctor starting the process, as did she. My results came back in a timely manner but hers seemed to take a bit longer. I placed a pause on going out, using various lackluster reasons, hoping to get the results of her test before moving forward *(because I knew the next date had a high percentage of clothing optional).*

I was at work when she called a few days later. She was quite upset. She was crying and she explained that she had tested positive. She wanted to meet in person and review the results after she consulted with her doctor. I agreed and we met. We reviewed the results together and she was shocked and embarrassed by them. She was devastated, and it had an impact on me. I felt bad but, in a way also relieved. It was one of those situations where even though it was rough it turned out okay.

Life isn't over if you have an STI/STD!

After a long conversation, we decided being friends was best, and we remained friends for quite some time afterwards. She decided to move on after finding a dating group where members had or were okay with STI's/STD's.

> Example dating sites for positive STI/STD
>
> - Positive Singles https://www.positivesingles.com/
> - MPWH https://www.mpwh.com/

The X

Sooner or later the X conversation will come up. Some of you may be lucky enough to have some pleasant ex-relationship stories, and if you are, then consider yourself blessed and either skip to the next section or keep on reading and send the rest of us some moral support. Because for the majority of us, one or both will soon be asking if the other's X is stalker, or perhaps even a violent type, lurking in the bushes. If you have children, then the dreaded family court debacle comes into play. This is a complex topic that would require a full book to even get started. If you have, or you are currently experiencing this now, I sincerely send you good vibes. Pandemic B.S. with family court over-lording can only add a mountain of stress. But enough of that depressing shit. Let's jump into a funny story about this and hopefully make you laugh a bit, shall we?

The X and Dog Shit Show

My X decided it was a good idea to move into a house one street over from where I currently lived at the time. It was awkward but, the kids could walk back and forth so that was her reasoning. Of course, you can imagine it wasn't my ideal living location situation. My X was a very lovely woman who felt the need to walk her dog in the morning right past my house. I found it very fascinating that she was able to train her pit bull to poop in my yard on a daily basis. I had no idea that she was so good with animals. Perhaps I had overlooked her dedication. Either way, I tried to laugh it off and ignored her. Looking back, I should have been more attentive but, alas, I failed. I had met someone new and it was going quite well. I had shared the fact that my X had moved close by and that she sometimes could be a tad, shall we say, uppity. Even with that out there, the new relationship progressed until the day in question. It was a memorable night as my girl and I had not seen each other in a few days. The relationship had developed into talking about a future. As the morning arrived, we were off to start the day. I opened the garage, and my X was there with her dog mid-poop in the front yard. I can still remember it like it was yesterday. The cold chill along with the smell of dog poop lingering in the air. My X called out, "Hey, new girl huh. What happened to the blonde the other day?"

This of course was not true, and my X knew it. But my current non-blonde girl was taken down a few pegs in that instant. I fumbled to respond, reeling from what my X had just said. I only added gasoline to a smoldering fire. "Just Ignore her" I said. My X giggled as her dog finished his business, and then she dropped a bomb that I would not recover from, calling out to my girl. "Honey, why do you think I have my dog shit on his front yard every morning? He did the same thing to me… you have a great day now."

And with that she walked away. I tried to reassure my girl, but my X was quite convincing. The bomb went off devastating my relationship. Oppenheimer himself couldn't have done a better job with that nuke.

I can laugh about it now, but at the time I wasn't. I was distracted and it was my downfall. Why was she having her dog shit on my yard every day you ask? Because we were having fun in family court. I volunteer this story to highlight that bitter X's do crazy things. Even more crazy if children are involved. Stay frosty…

Social Media

So many posts, so little time. Social media isn't going away any day soon but it sure can help out in different areas. It can keep you connected to far away friends and family, as well as to all kinds of fun. Yeah, in this pandemic it also offers a delusion of reality. Being locked away it's easy to gravitate to endless scrolling to relive boredom or fill in the holes of human interaction. My experience with social media has been mixed but I know it works for other people. With videos, news links, false information, deep fakes and a boatload of other things to encounter I'm advocating you Doom Scroll less… I have a few tales to get this across, but social media woes could be a separate book in itself regardless of this awesome pandemic.

My cautionary tales are of identity theft and

stalking. When I set up my social media accounts, I used my regular email address and volunteered too much information. Yep, I didn't know how easy it would be for bad actors to get all of my data. Another tragic tale of woe.

My friends list was growing to a level where I couldn't possibly keep up and I found that entertaining at times. I'm almost certain that others found that helpful, too, as I became a target for *'hacker's R Us'*. Yes, I didn't even know it, but those guys from Evil Corp sifted through my left-over posts and pieced together my habits. They used all of that goodness in their efforts and they were successful. I didn't have a clue until eBay was sending nasty grams my way. Those bad actors I spoke of... well they created an account with my email address and were selling very nice items on eBay in my name. Unfortunately, they weren't sending the items to the purchasers. This of course turned into quite a mess, until I also discovered that my LinkedIn account was spamming people. This scaled out to my utilities almost getting shutoff. I logged hundreds of hours on the phone sorting out accounts, and getting the passwords changed. Hence why security, privacy settings and password strength are strongly recommended.

Now, this next tale can be summed up as a social media stalker. Have you ever had that X that was deep in your circle of friends and, when you stopped dating them, they just kept hanging out with the group? Well, I watched this happen time and time again to some of my friends. The X would use the friends of friends feature on social media and miraculously be at the same events they were. It was a never-ending, drama-rama, merry-go-round. The only way to stop it was to reduce the friends list or seriously filter posts, etc. Things would eventually blow up and one of them would leave the circle of friends in a '*not good*' way.

I don't have an answer on how to prevent this, but it somehow relates to another of my mom's sayings, *"Don't dip your pen in the company ink"* Or alternatively stated, don't date within the group unless both parties agree on who is leaving if the relationship doesn't work out.

Safety tip: I mentioned getting hacked and yeah, it seems that it won't happen, but rest assured it can. Check your phone privacy settings and keep your friend list tight. Don't share too much info and for goodness sake don't upload all these awesome pictures of yourself. Someone else will use them for catfishing, cause you're hot, duh!

Bi-Nuclear or Blended

If you have children, then this section is for you. If you don't have kids but may be planning on dating someone who does, this section is worth a quick read. I'm sure by now finding someone you enjoy dating and who gets along with your children is a tall order right? Now, let's add that next level shit. No, the pandemic is another level up after this… Do your children get along with them and their children? Is your parenting style the same? Yeah, I know I'm not that good with math either, so calculating those odds are rather daunting. But hey, it happens, or at least that's what people say.

I have heard myself and friends ask, *"When do I introduce my kids to so-and-so?"* Well, this is further jacked up now with COVID. Pre-COVID there was so much advice out there on the *'what to do'* scenario that I was already lost, and let's face it, remote school learning with Zoom doesn't make parenting any easier. Who wants the joy of emails about their child not paying attention to class when they are sitting in the living room right? Now add this in with some family court drama, a pissy X and voila, you have a shit show beyond comparison. Thanks, COVID. So, when you are tabulating that *'want'* list, factor in the possibility of a partner's children.

Yeah, okay I'm designated **'Captain Obvious'** here, but there are ways I have found to navigate this loveliness. Now, keep an open mind because the suggestions here are just that… suggestions.

- Focus on you and build a solid foundation for the relationship you're wanting first, before you add the children into the mix. If it's right, that part will hopefully work out. And keep in mind that children grow up, especially teens. So, try not to pass on a good partner match because they might not get along with the children at first. And remember, tensions are higher now during the pandemic.

- If you're in it for a shorter-term relationship, then patience along with inevitable scheduling is key. Even booty calls will have to be scheduled around kids' school functions, X drop-offs, pickups, etc. Be prepared to have high intensity meetups that pack a lot of intimacy in a small window of time. Stay hydrated!

- If you're going to date someone with children, be okay with getting canceled on, rain check issued and shutdown due to children scheduling conflicts, etc. Children get sick, have emergencies and are generally joy killers when you're trying to date or hookup. *(Yeah, that sounded bad, but you know I'm right.)*

- If you get past all of these checklist items as well as the **DTR** *(Define the Relationship)* and you both are in agreement to place the kids in the mix, relax. First, high-five each other, you both made it together through that next level shit and you are making it work. Next, determine the best way to move forward knowing that you have time. For fucks sake, don't rush it.

Sly Fox, Get the Data

Foxes are known to be clever, but why? If you do some research, many folklores can be referenced containing fox tales. The tales describe the fox using more brains than brawn to get the job done. In a similar way, the same can be said about the difference between hunting versus fishing. Hunting is typically described as stalking your prey, whereas fishing uses a lure technique to catch them. So, female fox (vixen) or manly fox, use your cunning skills and lure your date to give up the data you need to meet your *'want'* list. I'll assume that you have found a few potentials that you would like to *'get to know'* shall we say? But before you meet John/Jane Doe at the local hangout, let's get some data.

Being sly can be many things, but as time is a factor, being bold in a sly way can be just as effective. Whether you're exchanging emails, texts or phone calls, consider taking notes. No, this isn't a spy novel where you're creating a dossier, but rather a quick reference that you can look back on. In an earlier section we reviewed the STAR technique. The note taking technique builds upon this. If you're treating this like a job interview, jotting down notes on the resume is customary.

How is this any different? Now, you may think this is a tad over the top, and true it could be viewed that way. Then why do it? Here are a few good reasons.

- You are planning on interacting with more than one person while dating. How do you organize the data obtained? Otherwise, you're gonna mess up and say the wrong shit to the wrong person! Yeah, I've done that... awkward.
- You want to note potential red flags and use follow up questions in the next conversation. *(Just like the cops do in those detective shows, ask the same question in a different way. Be clever.)*
- The other person may likely have implemented this technique and have detailed notes on you. *(You can bet your ass they are taking notes on you and others.)*

Your cunning skills hopefully have already begun by searching their social media footprint. Don't forget to search other dating platforms, too. Jeez, this is a lot of work. How can this help? Multiple profiles on dating sites raises questions. Especially if the profiles vary on describing themself and/or the pictures they've posted. Social media could indicate they already have a partner or worse, they are married. Their social media presence may be superman macho or hot playboy model, showing examples of partying last week in Mexico, deep sea diving with the sharks, bordering on unbelievable. Or they could be an overactive political commentator, which may be concerning if you do not share the same views. And don't forget to check LinkedIn, especially if they tell you who they work for!

In this pandemic wonderland, getting the data and organizing it will pay off dividends. Trust me. Yeah, okay, but still, I'm short on time; is there a faster way to disqualify someone? Yep, it's called the background check and its covered in the next section.

Background Checkup

In the days of Pre-Covid it was a good idea to do a background check on potential dates, but in a pandemic, it's strongly recommended. Why? Well depending on your *'want'* list, the background check could reveal red flags that are deal breakers for you. Some examples of deal breakers could be a massive criminal record, financial ruin, or data indicating a false identity. Either way, it's best to have the data if you're planning on doing more than watching movies online together. But how do I do a background check on someone you ask? Well, it's not as in-depth as a job background check per se, but websites offer data on individuals for a fee. A fee? Yep, you gotta pay, and if that bothers you a bit, ask yourself how much would you pay to get out of a mess? It's very similar to getting an Uber while heavily drinking instead of driving and getting a DUI or worse. Planning ahead is smart and safe, and so is the background check. There are quite a few sites that offer this service. I've used some and they have provided quite a bit of useful information on individuals.

Keep it to Yourself for a Bit…

There is a downside to knowing the data, and to volunteering that you know that data. My Paris story highlights this topic well. I had recently met this very nice woman and we had enjoyed a few dates together. The dates had gone well but we were still in the beginning phase of getting to know you. She had mentioned she was finally going on her dream trip to Paris. We had talked about it a few times and she would gush about how much fun it was going to be. She explained that she was traveling with her parents along with her children, but that she would be back in two weeks' time. She expressed interest in hopefully picking up from where we had left off and I agreed. I bid her farewell and went about my normal routine anticipating her return.

A week had gone by and I was checking the mail. To my surprise a postcard from Paris was in my mailbox. She had mailed me a postcard, signing it with a *"miss you, see you soon"* ...and, yet, I had never given her my home address! This really creeped me out, and it instantly made me wonder what else she had spied on me about. My mind whirled with thoughts of her invading my privacy and the likes. I had a hard time with it, and I decided not to continue dating her after she returned from Paris.

This could have been handled better by me, as well as her. If you are ever in a situation like this. I recommend you wait until you are further along in the relationship before acknowledging you have acquired data. Or not mention it at all… There can be a fine line between stalker and proper planning for safety. When in doubt, use caution.

Red Flags

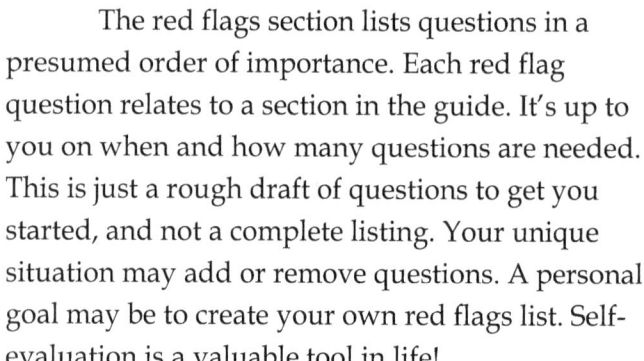

The red flags section lists questions in a presumed order of importance. Each red flag question relates to a section in the guide. It's up to you on when and how many questions are needed. This is just a rough draft of questions to get you started, and not a complete listing. Your unique situation may add or remove questions. A personal goal may be to create your own red flags list. Self-evaluation is a valuable tool in life!

Note: **If you feel unsettled with that new someone, just bail. Blocking is okay in today's world. Trust your instincts, safety is ALWAYS top priority!**

1. How colorful is your past?
    a. See background checkup.
    b. Are you a felon?
    c. Have you been incarcerated?
2. Are you currently *legally* married?
    a. Separated? See drama factor.
    b. Have you been divorced, and/or experienced family court?
    c. Are you dating someone now?
3. Do you enjoy recreational drugs – Ones not prescribed by your physician?
    a. Do you drink/smoke?

b. See PADTFM section.
4. When was the last time you were tested for STI/STD?
   a. See STI/STD section.
5. Can you tell me about your last relationship?
   a. See X section.
6. Do you enjoy firearms?
   a. See **PADTFM** section
7. Did you read the news? Do you agree/disagree with what's going on in the world?
   a. What are your thoughts on safety precautions of the pandemic?
   b. See **PADTFM** section
8. Do you miss Vegas. Do you gamble? What's your favorite game?
   a. See Vegas Baby section
9. Can you tell me about your occupation?
   a. See personality test/STAR.
10. Can you tell me about some of the things you enjoy?
    a. See transparency types section.

We Actually Do Shit

In this section of the survival guide, we list techniques to get the data needed before you unleash your cunning fox powers. This may seem like stalking your prey before the hunt but I tend to think of it as proper planning. There are some initial setup steps that will allow you to obscure your identity before you register on any of the dating sites. Why should you do this? Because bad actors are out there, plain and simple.

Mom saying here, "*Proper planning prevents poor performance!*"

Okay, picture corny sitcom dating advice scene setting with the main character saying, "*Have you ever Googled yourself?*" Now back to reality and focus. Seriously, if you haven't done it yet then you need to. Why? Because that's exactly what they will be doing at some point. It might be good to know what's out there before they ask you. Then you can hopefully have a great explanation for that crazy Vegas picture, or maybe simply adjust your privacy settings and/or delete it. I can almost bet your gonna say out loud, **"*No Fucking Way…*"** when you find shit out there… This is called the self-check step.

Self-Check

1. Google yourself. Try different combinations using your name, city, state, phone number, place of employment, etc. Then try your family members and see if/how they track back to you.

2. Check your credit score using your bank or other trusted financial institution. Place a lock on accounts that are not often used and set limits with email verifications if possible. The goal is to know your current situation before anything changes.

3. Recheck **ALL** of your privacy settings on **ALL** of your computer browsers and phone. Include your Amazon account, LinkedIn account, You Tube and all other social media accounts. Delete/Archive any old accounts, pictures, videos, events older than 6 months to a year. You no longer need them, and they can be easily used to show favorite places or behavior patterns. And while you're in there, do you really need that many friends? Time to weed out the distant friends, X's or non-essential contacts.

4. If you use the same password on multiple sites, first, slap yourself. Then change them. If you must use the same passwords on multiple sites, separate them into categories and don't mix and match. Example, your FB account password could be the same one for your library card, but not your bank account.

Note: ***Try to make your passwords as long as possible. If you can get to 10+ characters you're doing good. If possible, add your phone (text) as an extra verification step.***

5. Verify your address at the department of motor vehicles has a '*do not share*' checked for third parties. If you want full protection, get a mailbox at the Post Office or a UPS store and update your driver's license to use that address. This way anyone running your license plate or viewing your ID (Walmart/ bouncer at club) will have that address instead.

6. Create a new email address using Google Gmail and use it just for dating. Use a version of your name but, not your full name (**not your initials please**). This further insulates you from social media searches that will find you with a known email.

7. Also check your phone provider on what name appears on caller ID and if they have options for making your name private. *(IPhone has this feature, too.)*

8. View your profile on a background check website *(see Background Checkup section earlier in the guide)*. Examine how many people with your name and age range live in your city, etc. Bad actors may be able to narrow you down with a search. This may also influence your new email name.

9. If you have a LinkedIn account and you are secure in your job, set it to "*private*". It's easy to track back a name based on the company you said you worked for. Setting your profile to private may be difficult if you are in marketing or sales. I recommend saying you work for a local marketing company. Specifics on data can be vague when you are first meeting someone new. Always error on the side of caution. It's okay to say to a potential partner *"I'll share more as we get to know each other better."* If they push that might be a red flag. *(Consider using a low-resolution image /or none at all for*

LinkedIn. It's about your skills not what you look like…)

Google Voice

Hopefully you have created a new email address with Google Gmail outlined in the step six of the self-check section above. Using that email create a Google Voice number. This will allow you to have phone conversations using the Google number and not your real phone number, further insulating you. After you acquire the Google number, test it out with a friend, then update your social media contact number, as well as LinkedIn.

https://voice.google.com/about

To follow up, if big brother privacy is a concern, then you may want to limit your Google Voice number to persons you're filtering. Google Voice tracks just about everything. Considerations like call logs, voice mails, and other data should be reviewed. Also note that when you call/text a person, they now have your number. So, plan ahead for conversations, perhaps Zoom without video, etc. (*or just block your number when calling them back.*)

Pictures

Images, pictures, and videos are immortal on the internet. When you Googled yourself, did you check the images section? If not, you may want to recap the self-check section again. If you don't need your social media profile to have a picture, then remove it using the default picture. Some people like to use animals for a default. That's okay but, don't use your pet. Get a photo from the web that doesn't look like your fur baby at all. Remember the goal is anonymity. Now, if you already have images on the internet and they don't track back to you, feel free to use them in your online dating profile. If they do track back to you, avoid posting them on your dating profile. If you do, you risk voiding all of the work you just did. Keep public images posted on your social media presence to 5 or less. Avoid the tagging scenario… avoid sexting with your face in the image, duh!!! Avoid exchanging pictures in general until you know who it really is that you're sending pictures to… remember digital photos are immortal. (*This includes family pictures, kids, fur babies etc.*)

Dating Sites

It seems that the choices are endless, but one fact separates them, cost. If your *'want'* list details a longer lasting relationship with substance, a free site may not provide what you desire. In this scenario a pay site may be better suited. When you see they have paid to join a site, a few things can be assumed. First that the site owners have a payment card on file listing a name, address and other identifiable information that local law enforcement can subpoena if required. It also gives the impression that they are serious about a relationship. Keep in mind they could still be catfishing etc. as being an asshole is not against the law.

The Profile

What to write, huh… Saying things like: *'my friend is making me do this'*, *'…long romantic walks on beaches'* or *'I've never dated online before'* are not recommended. You need to write the profile, not your BFF or family. Be yourself, understand your audience, and know the type that you're trying to attract. If you're looking for steamy Vegas romps, flash some skin and keep the dialog to a minimum. If you're looking for the opposite, don't write a book. Instead, use your cunning to lure, while not being too restrictive. Finding the right balance between sexy and intriguing works every time. Adding a full pose from head to toe is recommended. People are visual creatures and they are going to find out what you look like eventually. Even if you get a few bad apples, don't despair, use them as practice to refine your technique. A catch and release system, if you will. Be ready to kiss more frogs until a prince/princess arrives.

Tip: *Don't use your full name or real initials. Try not to mention you're from (location) originally, or similar things that can easily identify you.*

Social media research

I'm assuming you have now cleaned up your profiles and your already on a dating site that, hopefully, will provide you with the results you desire. Now it's time to do to your potential date exactly what you protected yourself against. Google search, and then search again. Look for those nasty catfishing losers and other bottom feeders that are out there lurking. I'm sure you can find at least one of those hot guy/gal pictures on Google. If you suspect any shenanigans, don't engage, just move on. Karma is a bitch.

Communications

Yay, you have established a dialog with a potential partner. Woo Hoo! Now take a step back. Pretend all of your data lives in a swimming pool and the only way it gets out is via a garden house. This visual will help remind you to only let so much data out when you're emailing, texting, skyping, etc. You and your data are special and should be closely guarded. Wait until you are confident your new flame is not a whack job before volunteering more data about you or your life. We've all seen the dating shows where someone spills the beans and the other person uses that information against them. Either they do bad things with it or use it to manipulate the other person, all while you scream at the television in protest. Simply said, don't be that person. Trust your gut.

Note: You should be keeping mental notes during these times. Use those cunning skills to circle back to ask questions on the data they volunteered.

Video Chat

Everyone says, just do a video chat and then you will know. Uh, know what? I always respond. Video can be tricky, first we will assume you have completed some initial research. Even more so, that you have exchanged some texts or emails along with a phone call. All of that has gone well without any red flags or warnings. Then you may be ready for a video chat. But wait a minute, think about this a bit before you just click okay. Be safe, as always. Secure the room. What? Secure the room? Yep, that's what I said. Just as you insulated your phone, email and controlled your data release. Do the same for your surroundings. This is easily done by hanging a few sheets over where you are going to sit and in the background. Why? Well unless you have a completely empty room, people have stuff that tells a lot about them. Story time.

The Wrong Impression

Imagine you are participating in a video call with a perspective employer. It's the job you have been searching for. As you ace the questions, the interviewer notices something that they find offensive in the background. Either on the wall or perhaps placed on the desk where you are seated. You are unaware that this has occurred but a bias without context could result. Little did the interviewer know that your internet connection was under repair so you went to the neighbor's house to do the interview. It's too late, the seed has been planted to where the interviewer has lost concentration on you, but rather focused on the item in question instead. If you secure the room, you control the focus of the viewer, on you of course.

Now, reverse this shit. Use this exact technique if they don't secure the room. Look for pictures, objects and other tell-tale signs that will reveal more about them. If they have all of this awesomeness on display in clear view, that may be another insight into their personality.

If you decide on having online sex video

action with a person, first, I commend your bravado and I say have fun. One thing to note is that some people may record video sessions, and uh, that may not be your intention to share with others. In addition to that, others could hijack the feed. To limit your exposure, remember to secure the room, then limit your facial recognition with a playful mask or control the camera manually so that your face never shows. If you have sleeve tattoos or other easily identifiable marks you may choose to cover them as well. It all depends on your comfort level on the risk of your family viewing the video online. By then it's too late, you are a star!

In-Person

If you are moving right along with this potential partner, and an *'in-person'* meeting is scheduled, be smart. Not just because it's a pandemic but because bad shit really happens *(To guys and gals)*. Meet in a public place during the day, perhaps a coffee shop. Here are some super spy things to note.

- Masks? Hand sanitizer? That's up to you.
- Tell someone who/when/where you're going to meet. Setup the save me, escape call.
- Be familiar with the area, locate the exits, and the bathroom.

- Yes, other people should be in the coffee shop, hopefully social distancing.
- Make sure the parking lot where you park is easily seen. Not a parking garage.
- Take a different route home or stop at a store/friend's house prior, too.

Wow, really? That seems excessive. Yep, it probably is but remember they are just tips based on what I've heard and seen. One of my mom's saying sums it up best *'Safety is like an insurance policy; you pay upfront hoping to never need it.'*

After the In-Person (Long Term Size Up)

I'm assuming you have met in person and you and your new significant other are getting quite cozy. What do you do? Are you're looking for that long-term relationship and you're not sure if the new person will work out? Well, I think you already know what your gonna do... nothing! The *'hope is a method'* mantra hasn't been working out so well. Magically waiting to figure it out over time could be a factor in a pandemic. And uh, you're not getting any younger. Perhaps I could suggest another technique or two that could be useful.

Technique 1 – The Mini Vacation

If you have been cooped up in your living space for days due to COVID, then try taking a mini vacation. In short, get a hotel room for the weekend in the next city over. This can help prepare you for close quarters cohabitation with nowhere to go and nothing to do scenario (*Hello Pandemic!*). It's a non-stop eat, fuck, TV, shower, re-run. If you can make it for days sharing the same bathroom in that tiny room without arguing, then you may still be in the honeymoon phase or you have found that perfect partner. In the case of the honeymoon phase… you really should bicker over the trash pilling up from take-out or room service while you wrestle for the TV remote. Why? Couples will eventually fight over something. Learn early on how to disagree and compromise on things.

- Learn about each other's bathroom habits. Ya know, hair in the sink. Piss on the toilet. Not putting the seat down. Makeup and hair care products everywhere. Shit like that… then sort it out.

- Possession of the TV remote control tells you all about your partner's control level and their willingness to share with you. Sharing the remote and agreeing on shows is the ultimate partner relationship.

- Snoring, sleep schedule, cover hog, morning breath, and all the other real joys of being together with that special someone.

- Take note of financial willingness to pay or share the cost. Where you dine plays a part into what they told you versus what you experience in regard to spending habits. Review the financial section a few pages back if in doubt.

Technique 2 – Two Cooks in The Kitchen

Hey, we all have to eat, and this is a perfect opportunity to work together. If by chance your partner thinks this is stupid, ask them what they plan on doing instead of the cooking? Perhaps washing all the dishes? Truth told, take-out or dining out every night isn't a viable option in a pandemic, even if you are loaded with cash. The obvious thing you both learn is what type of food you prefer and each other's level of cooking expertise. It could be that one of you is an expert whereas the other has difficulty with toast. Yeah, that's totally me… so, how is cooking together gonna help? Let's list it out!

- Kitchens are usually tight quarters; you can see how well you move together in unison to prepare the meal and get the job done. Sneaking a kiss, slapping that ass or holding hands while you cook is fun, too. It's a great way to practice foreplay as well. You're not just heating up the water to a boil.

- Timing is key when cooking, along with prepping food. When couples learn to cook together, they can coordinate on other aspects of the relationship. It's a team building exercise and you want to know if your partner is team YOU.

- Enjoying what your effort produced is a reward in itself. Coming together and completing the task can really help build a strong foundation for the relationship to grow on. It also sets you up for great dessert options.

Technique 3 – Holiday Spirit

Yep, the holidays sneak up every year. To some peeps they decorate all year round but for others, hardly ever. This technique adopts the team process similar to the cooking team technique. The main goal is for you and your partner to setup/install holiday decorations or help others do the same with their holiday decorations. Holidays are filled with emotions and usually involve family. Involving your partner with the holidays is a great way to see if your partner is ready for you and your family.

- Setting up decorations may or may not involve family, but it does offer great communication channels for you to get to know each other better. Talking about childhood memories or movies you watched in the past around these times can keep the conversation going.

- Teamwork, patience and overall time sharing adds to the relationship foundation. If your family is involved, you can witness interactions and elicit feedback on your special someone. Or better yet, watch your family torture them for fun.

- Clearly the next holiday continues the tradition and hopefully sets the relationship up for future holidays being together.

Now let's jump into some areas that I use for my silly formula and light it up.

Work the Formula

Working the formula is just that. The formula is based on your *'want'* list with a few added extras to factor in. It's meant as a scaffolding to vent your list out in the open. When people write things down, things can suddenly become clearer than if we keep it all in our head. Remember, this is for fun and it's meant for you to get to know YOU better. After all, survival is the most <u>important</u> factor here. Let's turn the gears and see what happens.

Did you get your list created? Did you add the factors that were important to you? If you chose not to add a few of the factors, or you just weren't sure, that's okay. But please don't use a zero. Go with a 5 or lower as a default number. Using our examples, I've added some numbers. Your list may look entirely different and that is to be expected. Let's review the first one.

- I want the white picket fence family dream with someone.
    - Who likes with my children? **(1)**
    - Who doesn't have more than 2+ children? **(2)**
    - Who must like my dogs, or better yet...? My dogs must like him **(1)**
    - Who can BBQ, I don't want to go out all the time? **(3)**
    - Whose political affiliation needs to be at least close to mine **(1)**

- ✓ Drama Factor - 7
- ✓ Grey Area - 3
- ✓ Manners Factor - 6
- ✓ Health – 6
- ✓ Vegas Baby – 4
- ✓ Hot Mess – 3
- ✓ Hygiene Anyone – 5
- ✓ Financial Savvy -6

Now in this example. I reviewed the list and the priorities assigned to the list items. I contemplated and then selected the numbers for the sections. I did that assuming the list represented a long-term relationship. Now I want to walk through the sections, one by one, and provide some of my reasoning.

Drama Factor: I selected a seven due to the possibility of children on both sides, fur babies and dreaded X's. It's not that you want a level seven but it's probably what you're gonna get anyway. Being realistic helps.

Grey Area: I selected a three for good communication purposes, as well as I have yet to meet anyone who appreciates ass fuckery.

Manners Factor: I went with a six due to just living in this pandemic time warp can impact you in a way that may not be the norm. So, you or your potential partner could change Post-COVID.

Health: I chose a six with the hope your partner isn't going to need medical attention when you're fucking your brains out, after the children have finally fallen asleep. But your partner may have a few health issues.

Vegas Baby: I thought a four would be good. Hopefully the in-laws will allow the couple to get a weekend getaway going every now and then.

Hot Mess Factor: I went with a three, but I'm kinda undecided. This could go either way. Angel by day, devil at night comes to mind.

Hygiene Anyone: I picked a five due to single parenting, children and multi-tasking with work, COVID, etc.

Financial Savvy: I selected six for this section. I'm assuming there could be some issues with divorce or COVID related bullshit.

Formula Here

Do you recall when you were young, and you played that game with the paper folded up that had silly sayings on each of the fingers. The item in question is known as an origami fortune teller. *(you can find how to make one online).* Well, this is like that, only with more math. Similar to back then, we're still making shit up here.

Disclaimer: NASA did not contribute to this formula.

Oh, for the peeps that will try to mess with the formula (Yeah, you know who you are…), if you entered in the max score per section, then the chances of success are zero. If you couldn't help yourself and decided zero was a good number, you might get a skewed result. Remember the exercise is meant to be fun while getting to know what you want, but while also managing your expectations. You can treat the formula outcome to a passing score in school. And yes 60% may be passing in some circles, but it will be a bumpy ride of a relationship. Eh, that may be fun too ha ha.

Deep Diving it…

The equation is (*your total/81*) * -100, Then add 100. Which should give you a general percentage of success. After that we factor in each section weight and you get a final total. Easy right? Using our example above we can go step by step:

Step One

We start with adding up your total. Zeros are no fun, c'mon have fun.

$$7+3+6+6+4+3+5+6 = 40$$

Step Two

Ok, we have a total from step one. Let's divide the total by the maximum score of 81.

Eight sections, ten being the highest score per section equals eighty. Eighty-one is the exception in highest score. (11 for Vegas Baby potential.)

$$40/81 = .49382$$

Step Three

Take your total from step two and multiple it by a negative 100. We can now refer to it as a percentage.

$$.49382 \times -(100) = -(49.4)\%$$

Step Four

Add 100 to your percentage from step three. Looks good so far.

$$-(49.4)\% + 100 = 50.6\%$$

Step Five

Now, here comes that next level shit of the formula. We add or subtract based on section. Our Success rate based on our initial calculation is currently 50.60% The next step is to go through each section.

Drama Factor: If the drama factor is (less than) 3 or (greater than or equal) to 8 subtract 10%

> *Example score was 7, so no change.*

Grey Area: If the grey area is (less than) 5 add 10% but if it's (greater than or equal) to 5 subtract 10%

> *Example score was 3, so add 10%. The success rate is now 60.60%.*

Manners Factor: If the manners factor is (greater than) 5 add 10%

> *Example score was 6, so add 10% The success rate is now 70.60%.*

Health: If the health section is (greater than) 5 subtract 10%

> *Example score was 6, so subtract 10%. The success rate is now 60.60%.*

Vegas Baby: If the Vegas baby section is (greater than or equal) to 6 subtract 10%

> *Example score was 4, so no change.*

Step Five — Continued

Hot Mess: If the hot mess section is (greater than) 5 subtract 10%

> *Example score was 3, so no change*

Hygiene Anyone: If this section is (greater than or equal) to 5 add 10%

> *Example score was 5, so add 10%. The success rate is now 70.60%.*

Financial Savvy: The last section. If its (greater than) 6 subtract 10%

> Example score was 6, so no change.
> And the end total is 70.60%... not bad.

Alright, the first example looks like a decent outcome. Feel free to tweak the numbers and see how the results change. Okay, moving on to the second example. It's a bit different and that's to be expected.

- I want to stream movies with someone in safety
    - Who likes the same shows as I do? **(2)**
    - Who has a similar schedule as I do? **(1)**
    - Who is ok with talking on the phone while we watch? **(2)**

- Who *doesn't* talk during the show and interrupt the story line?**(3)**

- Who may be open to meeting in person in the future? **(3)**

✓ Drama Factor - 3
✓ Grey Area - 2
✓ Manners Factor - 4
✓ Health – 5
✓ Vegas Baby – 2
✓ Hot Mess – 5
✓ Hygiene Anyone – 5
✓ Financial Savvy - 2

In the second example. I reviewed the list and the priorities assigned to the list items. I quickly selected the numbers for the sections. This type of relationship could be short or long term. Still, I want to walk through the sections, one by one, and provide some reasoning.

Drama Factor: I selected a three due to the possibility of minor interruptions on both sides. It's the type of relationship where you don't want a lot of drama.

Grey Area: I selected a two for this section for constant rescheduling and the like. To me that's ass fuckery in the making. Stick to the schedule…

Manners Factor: I went with a four due to potential nose-picking, loud burping or outrageous flatulating during the show. Some might find this adding to the atmosphere; others may find it over the top offensive. I'll let you decide.

Health: I went with a default five due to it being an unknown factor in this made-up scenario. The truth is health isn't required. Just the ability to communicate somewhat effectively.

Vegas Baby: It was a two for me here. I doubt you will be traveling together but who knows these days.

Hot Mess Factor: I went with a five in this section. Maybe watching '*50 shades*' or other genres with a hot mess could help lead into other areas.

Hygiene Anyone: I went with a default five again. It's not required but, it would be nice if they were somewhat presentable if you were facetiming or Zooming while watching.

Financial Savvy: I selected two for this section. Hey, they at least gotta be able to afford a way to stream movies, right?

Using our second example, going step by step:

Step One

We start with adding up your total. Zeros are no fun, c'mon have fun.

$$3+2+4+5+2+5+2 = 28$$

Step Two

Ok, we have a total from step one. Let's divide the total by the maximum score of 81.

Eight sections, ten being the highest score per section equals eighty. Eighty-one is the exception in highest score. (11 for Vegas Baby potential.)

$$28/81 = .3456$$

Step Three

Take your total from step two and multiple it by a negative 100. We can now refer to it as a percentage.

$$.3456 \times -(100) = -(34.56)\%$$

Step Four

Add 100 to your percentage from step three. Looks good so far.

$$-(34.56)\% + 100 = 65.44\%$$

Step Five

Now, here comes that next level shit of the formula. We add or subtract based on section. Our Success rate based on our initial calculation is currently 65.44% The next step is to go through each section.

Drama Factor: If the drama factor is (less than) 3 or (greater than or equal) to 8 subtract 10%

Example score was 3, so no change.

Grey Area: If the grey area is (less than) 5 add 10% but if it's (greater than or equal) to 5 subtract 10%

Example score was 2, so add 10%. The success rate is now 75.44%.

Manners Factor: If the manners factor is (greater than) 5 add 10%

Example score was 4, so no change.

Step Five - Continued

Health: If the health section is (greater than) 5 subtract 10%

> *Example score was 5, so no change*

Vegas Baby: If the Vegas Baby section is (greater than or equal) to 6 subtract 10%

> *Example score was 2, so no change.*

Hot Mess: If the Hot Mess section is (greater than) 5 subtract 10%

> *Example score was 5, so no change.*

Hygiene Anyone: If this section is (greater than or equal) to 5 add 10%

> *Example score was 5, so add 10%. The Success rate is now 85.44%*

Financial Savvy: The last section. If its (greater than) 6 subtract 10%

Example score was 2, so no change. And the end total is 85.44%... no surprise having a streaming partner will usually yield a high success rate.

Now that we walked through two examples you can see that the numbers speak for themselves. In the *'We Actually do Shit'* section the topic of taking notes on individuals was discussed. Adding these calculation sections to the notes and putting in some initial numbers is a great way to finish detailing their profile. This allows you to review your options before you meet in person. Here is an example of a spreadsheet I created.

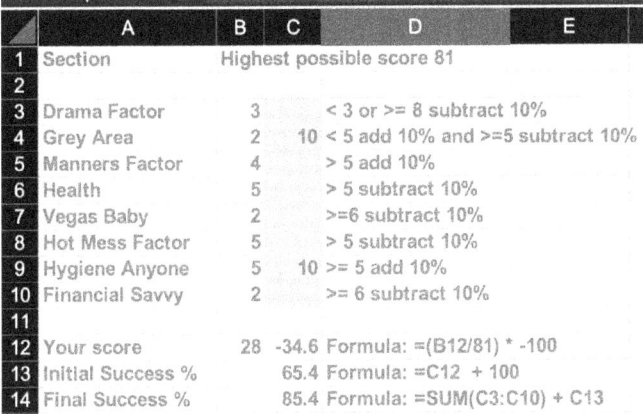

For real? You want me to create a spreadsheet and tweak some numbers? Not really, but you can if you want to. You can simply add it to your notes that you have been hopefully taking. The spreadsheet is a fun way to demonstrate a correlation between data. Clearly more drama and lying have an impact on the percentage of a good relationship. But if you just want a streaming friend the formula is rather obvious.

Wrap Up

Well, now is the time to realize that you may encounter a fox slyer than yourself. Yes, we have all been outfoxed a time or two. Don't feel bad; it happens. Learn from it and add it to your self-check list for next time. Don't be discouraged by jerks, bad apples or the many bad actors out there. It's a pandemic and being creative can get you through it. Just think the guys/gals living at home you avoided Pre-COVID may work out now. They are accustomed to being confined and have many in home activities they enjoy. Who knows they may still be there after COVID too? But I'll let you decide if that's a good or bad thing.

I hope you have picked up some useful tips as well as enjoyed some of the humorous stories. I'm sure you have countless stories of your own, and without them how can we hope to eventually find that person we are meant to be with.

As always be smart, be safe and good luck out there.

Time wasters for work

Try making one or more of these templates in your favorite at-office work program. It's a great way to waste time at work. Get crazy foxlike and create a way to gather and review potential partners. You can never have enough data. Why? Because its more organized than just daydreaming.

list of all lists - want list template example.

Overview your 'want' - EX: I want to stream movies...

Bullets that refine the overview EX: Who likes the same shows as me...

My Self checklist, I know you can add more to this lame template.

My Self Checklist   X

I really did Google myself.
I checked my credit and reviewed my finances.
I checked and then rechecked my privacy settings.
I verified ALL my passwords.
I reviewed my address and thought about a PO Box.
I created a new email address.
I checked my phone provider settings.
I reviewed my profile on a backgroud site.
I reviewed my LinkedIn and other social media.
I actually read something on Google Voice.

Lame dating terms of the New Millennium

Ok, it's time to review some of those new/not so new terms that are associated with dating. Because let's face it, ya gotta learn them sooner or later. And when you do, you will realize that some hipsters just categorized all the shit you and I have already experienced only they added some latte trendiness. It reminds me of texting LOL or something else clever instead of spelling it out. What's that all about? (*I can hear my kids saying, OK Boomer…as if!!!"*)

Ok, the terms are listed in alphabetic order. They could have been grouped together by type, but I found this easier to navigate. In addition to sort order some of the terms include other terms that are similar.

Example: term A is like term B etc.

Using the list of dating terms as a reference list was my intention. Try to enjoy them rather than dwelling upon them.

Breadcrumming

The term is described as sending out sassy/flirty/sexy but non-committal messages to keep a prospect/partner/or otherwise potential person on the hook by showing the minimum amount of interest. It's a Handsel and Gretel story of leaving a trail of breadcrumbs for someone to follow.

Benching

Similar to *breadcrumming* but, perhaps a bit further. Not yet ready to commit to officially dating the person, yet not wanting to let them to move on. They are benched on the sidelines with false hope they will play sooner than later.

Caspering - Soft Ghosting

Unlike traditional ghosting which involves no communication, 'soft ghosting' refers to one-word responses or using a formulated 'like', thumbs up, or emoji instead of replying in a meaningful way, in order to continue communication. If you remember the cartoon *'Casper the Friendly Ghost'* that's the irony. Caspering when dating isn't really friendly, it's actually kinda rude, ya know?

Catfishing

A mainstream term with a movie and reality TV

show to match, it describes a person perpetrating to be someone you are interested in, when in fact they are someone totally different. The use of false pictures and avoiding in-person meetings are key behavior trends.

Cause-playing

After a relationship/dating fails, the other person still contacts you about non-relationship events or to ask for a favor, hence furthering their own "cause". Typical scenarios may sound like this..." Hey my band is playing. Please come out and show your support!", or "Hey, can you help me move that red couch of mine?"

Cloaking

Similar to ghosting but next level shit. In addition to no communication, getting 'cloaked' includes unmatching, unfriending and being blocked on all apps. *C'ya*. At this point, the other person seriously doesn't want anything to do with you, for reasons you may or may not know.

Cookie-Jarring

Finding out they've been seeing someone else behind your back, while they have been keeping you benched. "Like my mom would say, *'They got caught with their hand in the cookie jar.'*"

Corona-zoned

This term denotes behavior of avoiding coming over to the person's place to meet/hook up/ or otherwise engage with in-person meeting out of fear of catching or spreading the virus.

Covidivorce

A rather obvious term where a marriage/separation occurs due to stress of lockdowns, quarantines, etc. Being locked in a space 24/7 with a significant other may be a pleasant experience for some, but for others it can lead to unhappiness and eventual breakdown of a relationship.

COVID-worthy

A new term, used to define if a potential date is of an acceptable quality to engage in dating during the pandemic. (Often interchangeable with the term "Apocalypse Partner".)

Cuffing (Cuffing Season)

The term defines singles getting into relationships for the colder months, when opportunities to date become more cumbersome due to weather.

Curved (Getting or being, AKA Curbed)

The awesomeness of being rejected, shot down,

dissed, dismissed, kicked to the curb, etc. Uh, not everyone is gonna like you, get over it.

Cushioning

The behavior of continuing to stay in contact with one or more present/past partners/love interests as backup. This can cushion the blow if the main person of interest fails to deliver.

Dateview (Date Interview)

Spending the entire first date asking serious question after question. Although I like this approach when dating, one should try to mix it up a bit to see if they actually enjoy the person.

Deepliking

Yeah, the creepy way of showing interest by scrolling backwards through their social media pictures and posts and liking them from months or even years before the two of you met. This behavior, in my opinion, is a red flag.

Dial-toning

Similar to ghosting but it describes ignoring the person before they even get a chance to be ghosted. Back in the day this was similar to giving out a bad phone number.

Digital Detoxing

Usually referred to as an escape from Doom Scrolling. The person uses this technique to discontinue communications when they are no longer interested. This provides an opportunity to return later without being labeled a *Ghost*, *Zombie*, *Submarine* or other term.

Dogfishing

Not to be confused with *catfishing*, where a person pretends to be someone they're not, in order to trick another into falling in love with them. Dogfishing peeps pretend to have a dog in order to relate to you <Sigh>. Some have even been known to borrow a friend's dog, visit the dog park, or post pics with a dog that isn't even theirs. Messed up, right?

DTR

Define The Relationship – it's an important thing in any relationship. DTR defines you and your partner's relationship, where the details are presented so that peeps can't say they didn't know shit later on. "Uh, yeah, I was thinking the relationship was open..." Fuck you.

Eclipsing

At times when dating, one party may adopt the

other persons hobbies. Which seems harmless and perhaps mutually beneficial at first. It turns awkward when the other person adopts multiple hobbies at full speed and therefore totally changes from the person they were when you originally met.

Ex text (COVID-edition)

An out-of-blue text sent to an ex because you're both living through a pandemic. The text is sent because the person misses "life before COVID" and is searching for comfort in a familiar situation. Even if they weren't as awesome as you wanted them to be, they are still better than today.

Exoskeleton-ing

Getting approached via social media/text/call by a current partner's ex. The term relates to your partner's skeletons coming out of the closet. I can't recall this being good unless you're teaming up to roast them in family court.

FBO

An acronym for making a relationship "Facebook official". I recommend the *DTR* prior to this in order to avoid embarrassment, among other things.

Flashpanning

Sometimes referred to as the Honeymoon period. Flashpanners live for that first few months of dating when the relationship is intense. You know, sex from chandeliers and such. As we all know that doesn't last forever, hence the term. Flashpanners, living for that excitement, tend to bail out after the Honeymoon is over only to repeat the cycle all over again with a new partner.

Flatlining

The common phenomenon that defines attempting to keep up a conversation with someone that isn't interested or just sucks at conversation. Hopefully this doesn't translate to their sexual abilities.

Fleabagging

Just like the TV show where the main character seems to pick unavailable/wrong partners. The term defines that scenario. If you're reading this book, you may have experienced this, too. ☐

Ghosting

To disappear out of someone's life because you're no longer interested in them, instead of telling them directly. One simply ceases all communication. Unfortunately, the ghostee is usually left hurt and confused. Uh, yeah like WTF, feedback helps the next person duh. How am I gonna grow as a person?

Firedooring

This term describes a form of one-way communication. Whereas you begin a relationship/conversation but as it continues, the communication is restricted to one way and usually not reciprocated. A firewall in computer works this way.

Glamboozled

Getting all dressed up for a date but they cancel on you last minute, similar to all dressed up and no place to go. The additional terms *Next On Deck,* or *Cushioning* come to mind...

Half-night stand

Yep, it's just like the one-night stand, minus the staying the night part. Other references to *'Netflix and Chill'* or *'Quarantine and Chill'*. I would call it a bump and grind session but hey, I'm old school. So, technically the late-night guest leaves straight after/shortly after the sex is over.

Haunting

This usually occurs after having finished things with a date that didn't go well or perhaps a prior failed relationship. You notice signs that your date/ex is looking/liking/commenting at your social media, going to your hangouts etc. It's a deliberate but scary attempt to remind you that they exist. Sounds like a stalker to me...

Jekylling

This behavior is known as the Jekyll and Hyde-type person. They have two sides to them. The first side is awesome when things are going great, but they quickly turn sour when things are not going well. Think Bi-Polar, yeah, we know this type don't we... Jekylling must be the politically correct way of saying they are bat shit crazy.

Kittenfishing

Defined as portraying yourself in an unrealistically positive light in your online dating profile. Glamor shots anyone? Kittenfishing crosses the border into dishonest ass fuckery, bait and switch bullshit, or flat out lying. Take caution; what else are they embellishing on?

Layby

A term associated with someone who is all about flirting, while they pursue better options in the fast lane. Similar to *benching*, *Cushioning* and dangerously close to '*Ass Fuckery*' behavior.

Love bombing

Described as when the new love interest shows extreme amounts of affection early on in the relationship to win you over. Unfortunately, after said winning, the game changes and the amount of affection subsides, and it has the potential to turn into a manipulative or abusive relationship. Love bombing is similar to *Flashpaning* but with more *Jekyllying*.

Monkeying

When you move from one relationship to the next without any time in between, like a monkey swinging from the branches of a tree. hey, I'm not judging.

Next On Deck

Kind of like waiting in the wings, having someone be 'next on deck' means they're a good option that you'll call up if your current thing doesn't work out. Similar to *Layby*, B*enching*, *Cushioning* but somewhat understandable in the dating world.

Obligaswiping

This odd term refers to the act of endlessly swiping on dating apps attempting to find a date when they may not really want one. They may participate to a certain degree, but it just seems to never get to hello. Almost fulfilling an obligation to themselves or others that they are trying.

Orbiting

Defined as that person who constantly watches your Instagram, Snapchat and likes all of your posts in hopes that you will notice them. Some people use this tactic on new or former dates/partners to let them know they're still interested. Similar to *Haunting* but they may never have had to chance to get with you yet... Perhaps they are now *Covid-Worthy*?

Peacocking

Dressing up for social media or even in real life, to gain attention. Can be sometimes combined with *Thirst Trapping* or just plain showing off.

Phubbing

The rude act of always being connected to the grid by means of a phone or other technological device when they are with you. This can usually be corrected with '*Yellow Carding*' or just simply agreeing to social norms prior to meeting.

Pocketing

Defined as seeing someone for a while but not meeting their friends or family. They seem to be keeping you on the down-low *'in their pocket'*. Similar to *Stashing*.

Quarantine bae'

A dating partner/love interest/or another person that you have tentatively agreed to see during the lockdown. The arrangement with this person may be complex and/or confusing.

Quarantine & Chill

Just like Netflix and Chill, Quarantine and Chill can mean hanging out with someone for the sole purpose of intimacy during this fucked up pandemic.

Roaching

The dubious player activity we have all experienced when dating. Clearly it sucks. *'Hate the game and not the player'* is a typical loser response you may have heard. Roaching unfortunately is common, messed up and definitely in the realm of *'Ass Fuckery'*. The *DTR* helps but not always. Cockroaches are single for a reason and they are usually accomplished liars. Caution, they are known to be clever survivors.

Rossing

I had to look this one up... "Recalling an episode of

Friends where Ross and Rachel take a break, and Ross goes straight out and hooks up with someone else" Who knew they had a term for that?

Slow Fading

Described as a kinder version of *ghosting*, where the person slowly reduces contact with the other person. Sometimes associated with *'breadcrumbing'* or version of the *'Digital Detox Cycle'*

Stashing

Similar to *Pocketing*, Stashing is usually taken a step further by failing to mention their existence even on social media.

Stealthing

I was taken aback by this term. Yep, there be rotten peeps out there. It refers to when a partner either lies about contraceptives or flat out covertly removes their condom during sexual intimacy (Get the fuck out!). See the STI/STD section.

Submarining

This term has been around for a while. It describes when an ex pops back up in your life after a lengthy period of time of being AWOL. It may or may not be useful depending on the circumstances. They could have the same ideas as you during this pandemic. (Timing is everything with submarining.)

Textlationship

A flirtatious communication via text/Skype/What's App/ etc. That just never goes anywhere else. Similar to *Layby*, *Cushioning*, *Benching*, or simply friend-zoning.

Throning

An expanding term for gold-digging that extends beyond wealth. It involves using another person for their power and/or social status, and it's most common when one person in the relationship has significantly less money or influence than their counterpart.

Tindstagramming

Contacting someone through Instagram's direct messaging (DM) after seeing them on Tinder. Hey, if they've already swiped left, then I doubt they want a DM from you, ya know?

Turbo relationship

A relationship defined as faster and more intense due to the pandemic. Pre-COVID relationships were usually spread out over more time, whereas Tubo relationships are condensed and move at record speeds. Caution again; twice as bright, half as long.

Type-Casting

This term describes the trend of only dating others based on their personality type, astrological sign, or other specific typed area. Personally, I find it a good practice, because you know what you like, but some may feel differently.

Uncuffing

Unfortunately, the direct opposite of *Cuffing*. You're getting dumped. Uh, yeah that sucked!

Virtual date

A date held on FaceTime, Zoom, or another web chat platform. Also has the slang term '*Vate*' associated with it. This is an excellent practice that is described in depth in the '*We Actually do shit*' section.

Virtual One Night Stand

Exactly like a Virtual date but it includes more intimate behavior. Caution: be safe and make sure you are not being recorded for replay to others.

Vultures

The term is descriptive in itself. Circling for the

chance to swing in and take advantage of someone in an incredibly weak and vulnerable state. Example, after you're dumped, they swoop in.

Whelming

Online dating can be a rainstorm or a desert. When you first get on, you may receive a lot of interest. This is great news but sharing that success with your dates isn't very nice. Someone might take it as being rude or boasting about your overwhelming options, hence the term.

White Clawing

The term defines continuing a relationship solely based on a favorable attribute whereas the rest of person is deemed undesirable. Usually associated with attractive persons that are dull or dim whited… our older generation knew it as simply being shallow.

Yellow Carding

If you are into sports this reference details the term. It simply is another description for calling out bad behavior during dating/relationships. I believe a red card calls the end of the relationship, game, set and match, so to speak.

Zombieing

When a ghoster suddenly resumes communication, they are returning from the dead as if nothing ever happened. Before smashing their brains out consider that the situation may have the potential to offer closure and/or feedback on why they ghosted you in the first place.

Zumped

Being dumped on Zoom, FaceTime, or another web chat platform. Because getting dumped via text is so 2000's.

Whew, we made it. Hopefully with these terms defined you can navigate the blogs and conversations better in the dating world.

Acknowledgements

Thank you.. to the countless number of friends, past dates and family that helped contribute to this book. Without your input, positive and negative, it would not have been possible.

I would like to give a special thanks to Rebecca Steinmetz for once again serving as my copy editor.

Cover picture from Unsplash 11-20 credits:
- birger-strahl-fOV7nWWIwRk-unsplash.jpg
- thomas-malik-jnaxkuTyoug-unsplash.jpg

All other artwork by RTG Books

This book of fiction was inspired by my personal life. All of the characters, names, businesses, locations and events have been fictionalized for dramatization purposes. Any similarity to the name, character of any person is entirely coincidental and unintentional.

www.ingramcontent.com/pod-product-compliance
Lightning Source LLC
Chambersburg PA
CBHW071515040426
42444CB00008B/1661